Arts and Crafts
EMBROIDERY

Laura Euler

Schiffer Publishing Ltd

4880 Lower Valley Road • Atglen, PA 19310

Dedication

To Josh and to Kelli

Other Schiffer Books by the Author:
The Glasgow Style: Artists in the Decorative Arts, circa 1900.
ISBN: 978-0-7643-3044-5. $69.99

Other Schiffer Books on Related Subjects:
*Silk Art Embroidery: A Woman's History of Ornament &
Empowerment.* Donna Cardwell. ISBN: 978-0-7643-2906-7.
$29.99
The Stitches of Creative Embroidery. Jacqueline Enthoven.
ISBN: 978-0-8874-0111-4. $24.99

Cover designed by: Danielle Farmer
Type set in P22 Arts & Crafts Hunter/Dutch 809 BT

ISBN: 978-0-7643-4409-1
Printed in China

Published by Schiffer Publishing, Ltd.
4880 Lower Valley Road
Atglen, PA 19310
Phone: (610) 593-1777; Fax: (610) 593-2002
E-mail: Info@schifferbooks.com

For the largest selection of fine reference books on this
and related subjects, please visit our website at
www.schifferbooks.com. You may also write for
a free catalog.

This book may be purchased from the publisher.
Please try your bookstore first.

We arc always looking for people to write books on new
and related subjects. If you have an idea for a book,
please contact us at
proposals@schifferbooks.com

Schiffer Books are available at special discounts for bulk
purchases for sales promotions or premiums. Special
editions, including personalized covers, corporate
imprints, and excerpts can be created in large quantities
for special needs. For more information contact the
publisher.

In Europe, Schiffer books are distributed by
Bushwood Books
6 Marksbury Ave.
Kew Gardens
Surrey TW9 4JF England
Phone: 44 (0) 20 8392 8585; Fax: 44 (0) 20 8392 9876
E-mail: info@bushwoodbooks.co.uk
Website: www.bushwoodbooks.co.uk

Contents

Acknowledgments

So many people kindly shared their time to help me make this book a success. I can't thank them enough.

First, thanks to the lovely ladies of the Seattle Arts and Crafts Guild who shared their fantastic collections with us: Kim Covey, L. Teresa Di Biase, Jessica Greenway, Faire Ferrill Lees, Lorrie Moore, and Jane Roe. Thank you to Jan Edwards for sharing her collection and thanks to Dianne Ayres for sharing hers. Thanks to Aurora Weiner for modeling.

Thanks to all the folks who helped out with images: Meg Andrews, Dianne Ayres, Paul Bailey, June Barrett, Mike Bascomb, Salah Ben Halim, Victoria Billington, Kajette Bloomfield, Anna Buruma, Ann Chaves, Karen Euler (hi Mom), David Ford, Martha Frankel, Sarah Gates, Fiona Grimer, Philip Hunt, Michael Jeffery, Peter King, John Mackie, Sara Meier, Natalie Paris, Patrick Rogers, Kerry Taylor, Ann Wallace, Dave Warren, Louis Webre, and Mildred Yuan.

And then, thanks to everyone who listened and advised during the writing of the manuscript: Stafford Waters, as always; Kelli Kirk, Debra Euler, and Martin Windram. Julian Trupin helped with the bibliography.

Unless otherwise stated, all photos in this book are copyright Joshua Trupin.

Introduction

Embroidered textiles are to me the most personal and immediate art form practiced by the Arts and Crafts Movement. Eighty to one hundred years after they were made, I can still easily see the craftswoman's hand in each piece. I even treasure the mistakes, the dings, the little holes, and tiny silk shatterings. These all prove that this is a piece of art from another time, which has its own story to tell.

I love that embroidery is almost universally feminine as an art: made by women, often designed by women, and treasured by women. Also, embroidery was quite possibly the way a woman supported herself and her family. These pieces may have been the only Arts and Crafts items in someone's humble home, made to express an aesthetic that, owing to finances, couldn't be manifested any other way. Some pieces are the humble workaday pieces for utility in the home, made to hold a whisk broom or decorate a luncheon table. Exceptional pieces may have been made professionally as works of art, only for display, by distressed gentlewomen who needed to earn their living by selling through ladies' work societies.

Here I will explore the British—English and Scottish—movements, as well as the American.

Unfortunately, an entirely global book is too broad of a scope for this book. One or two Irish, French, or German embroideries might sneak in, as I couldn't bear to leave them out. I'm not an academic, so don't expect an academic treatment with footnotes. Also, a lot of the Glasgow section is similar to the embroidery section in my book on the Glasgow Style. I'm just here to share some beautiful items and what I know of their histories with you. I do tend to use primary sources when possible; they're interesting and the writing is often quaint and fun.

This book is about surface embroidery only— not lace, not tatting, not anything else. Nor will I discuss how to embroider—there are tons of books about that, not to mention an Internet. I may also go off on little subject zigs and zags because I think they're interesting. Skip to the pictures if you don't like them.

First I will explain how the Arts and Crafts Movement came about, and then explore some common design principles. After that, I will go through the various stages of the movement in roughly chronological order.

Chapter 1

The Beginning of the Arts and Crafts Movement

It didn't begin with Pugin. It didn't begin with Ruskin. It began because of government action. The Industrial Revolution had established Britain as the manufacturing leader of the world. British products were sold around the globe. But in 1820, Parliament declared that free trade—the abolishment of all tariffs and duties—was to be the guiding principle of economic policy. Now British goods had to compete with foreign merchandise on an even field. It was felt that European products were better designed than British and Britain felt its economic power was at risk.

In 1835 the House of Commons appointed a Select Committee to "Enquire into the best means of extending a knowledge of the Arts and the principles of Design among the people, especially the manufacturing population of the country." The upshot was that countries such as France and Prussia had established schools of design and Britain had not. The Committee recommended that Parliament vote £1500 to establish a government school of design in London with others to follow in major cities. The schools of design would then enable British designers to improve the quality of their wares and increase foreign trade.

The first Government School for Design was begun in 1837; five years later one was started in Birmingham. The first Female School of Design was opened in 1842. The Government School for Design eventually (1853) became the National Art Training School with the Female School of Art in separate buildings; in 1896, it was renamed Royal College of Art. During the nineteenth century, the school was often referred to as the South Kensington Schools.

But the system of design schools was unpopular. May Morris wrote in 1906, "The unpopularity of the system is not surprising; it should have been foreseen that a designer of artistic instincts and artistic training cannot be turned out to order, machine-made, well-calendered and finished, like a bale of Manchester cotton."

Figure 1. Henry Cole memorial portrait. *Illustrated London News*, April 29, 1882.

After the Great Exhibition of 1851, the government set up a Department of Practical Art to oversee design education. Its superintendent was Henry Cole (see Figure 1), the organizer of the Great Exhibition. In 1852 Henry Cole put together a group of manufactured items from the Great Exhibition of which he disapproved, called False Principles of Design. At the Museum of Manufactures in South Kensington, which eventually became the Victoria

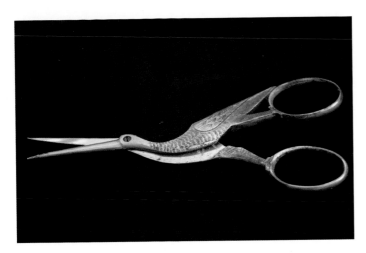

Figure 2. These scissors may look cute, but they're pure design horror.

and Albert Museum, each item, such as wallpaper with perspective drawing on it, was displayed with a label explaining why it was atrocious, which was explored in great detail in the catalog. (Don't you wish you'd gone to this exhibition?) The exhibition only lasted two weeks, because oddly enough the owners of the items in the "Chamber of Horrors," as it was known, objected to their being displayed there and withdrew their property.

The most egregious of the false principles of design was the ringing "Direct Imitation of Nature." A carpet should not look like a pond of water nor a field of flowers, because there should not be a pond of water in your drawing room nor a field of flowers. Wallpaper should not have perspective drawings of the Crystal Palace nor a railway station on them because walls should be flat. As the exhibition catalog noted, "There has arisen a new species of ornament of the most objectionable kind, which is desirable at once to deprecate on account of its complete departure from just taste and true principles. This may be called the natural or imitative style, and is seen in its worst development in some of the articles of form."

In 1876, the great designer Dr. Christopher Dresser (who, incidentally, attended the Government School for Design) recalled some of the contents of the Chamber of Horrors in a lecture about design later printed in *Penn Monthly*, Volume 8, 1877: "Thus we had scissors formed as birds, which separated into halves every time that the scissors were opened; candle-sticks formed as human beings, with the candle fitting into the top of a chimney pot hat or into the head; egg-cups formed as birds' nests; plaid fabrics bearing check patterns so large that it almost required two persons to wear the same pattern in order that the whole design be seen; carpets on which ponds of water were drawn with water-lilies floating upon them; and other absurdities equally offensive to good taste." Most of the items in the Chamber of Horrors went on to be best-sellers, and even 160 years later I'm pretty sure I have one of those bird scissors in my sewing box (see Figure 2). Sorry, Mr. Cole.

(By the way, Henry Cole was lampooned amusingly in Dickens' *Hard Times*. A guest speaking to Thomas Gradgrind's students asks them if they would "paper a room with representations of horses." When the students say sure, why not, the learned gentleman schools them about design. "You are not to have, in any object of use or ornament, what would be a contradiction in fact. You don't walk upon flowers in fact; you cannot be allowed to walk upon flowers in carpets. You don't find that foreign birds and butterflies come and perch upon your crockery; you cannot be permitted to paint foreign birds and butterflies upon your crockery. You never meet with quadrupeds going up and down walls; you must not have quadrupeds represented upon walls." Henry Cole was friendly with Dickens and took the portrayal in good spirits.)

Arts and Crafts Ideals

By the 1880s, artists and designers associated with the movement began to agree on principles that make a piece an Arts and Crafts design. Two of the guiding principles most applicable to embroidery are conventional design and truth to materials. What does that mean?

Conventionalization of design was something Arts and Crafts design critics spent a lot of time on: translating three-dimensional nature into a representation of nature, rather than trying to imitate it as closely as possible (**remember:** no direct imitation of nature or you'll have Mr. Henry Cole to answer to). Regularized and simplified natural forms were to be aimed for: a rose should look like a Tudor rose, or a Glasgow rose, not a three-dimensional rose with shading. Lewis F. Day wrote that conventional treatment should be "such a rendering of natural forms as may be consistent with the decorative character of art." Figure 3 shows conventional cinquefoil and daffodil designs by Walter Crane.

Therefore, an embroidered picture should look like what it is, an embroidered picture, not a painting, just as wallpaper should look like wallpaper, not a perspective rendering of a railway station.

May Morris stated in *Decorative Needlework* (1893), "You will have often heard the words convention and conventional used as opposed to naturalistic forms in a decorative design. Now, the first thing the designer will do is to go to natural growths and animal life, and show his pleasure in them by studying their infinite variety and beauty, and introducing them into his work. … But his own work should merely recall nature, not absolutely copy it … Whatever growth is chosen as a model will thus be represented by the draftsman's hand, but translated, as it were, and serving the purpose of giving delight almost as well as when growing in the fields: in exchange for the subtle, unconscious and untranslatable beauty of nature, we get the charm of conscious art …"

The next idea is truth to materials. If the embroidery is to look like embroidery, the innate quality of the materials used should influence the objects created from them.

Mary Lockwood and Elizabeth Glaister write in *Art Needlework*, "Needlework should be in every way adapted to the materials used. As the sculptor's chisel and the painter's brush have each their separate function and domain, so has the needle of the embroideress; nor should anything lying beyond its proper powers be attempted by its means. […] With regard to the imitation of flowers in needlework, it is evident that the imitation must be incomplete, and that less must be attempted than in painting. It is as impossible to reproduce the odor of flowers as it is to imitate the bloom of their texture, the delicacy and evanescence of their more brilliant tints, or the minute details of their form. The attempt must, once for all, be abandoned, and only those aspects of form and color be chosen which are capable of being adapted and combined so as to produce a satisfactory result in the manner called conventional. This limitation is imposed on our art by the nature of its materials, and follows from a just appreciation of what may be successfully accomplished with those materials."

Later, in 1903, Mackay Hugh Baillie-Scott, the designer and architect, wrote in *The Studio*, volume 28: "What are the effects to be obtained by the needle which are peculiar, characteristic, and essential, and which can be obtained in no other way? That seems one of the first questions to be asked. If it is necessary to compete with the painter, what can we achieve with the needle that he cannot achieve with his brush? There are many things. The sheen of silk, the glitter of jewels, the gleam of pearls, are not the least amongst them …"

Figure 3. Conventional flower designs by Walter Crane for embroidery. *Handbook of Embroidery*.

Needlework Before Arts and Crafts

In medieval times, English embroidery could be of astonishing quality and it was revered as art. While nuns and noblewomen did much embroidery, there were also quite a few professional embroiderers, both male and female. These professionals were usually employed in large workshops in London. The Syon Cope, which was much admired by Arts and Crafts embroiderers, was made by these professionals. Artists designed some embroidery, but much was also copied from illuminated manuscripts.

Over the centuries, needlework became devalued as women's work. As printing became cheaper, printed patterns for embroidery became more widespread. Embroidery was taught to girls as part of their education, but as a housewifely skill, not an art. Generally speaking, there were three types of embroidery: pictures, meant only for display on the wall; decorative work, on clothing or household goods; and samplers. May Morris, again from *Decorative Needlework*: "There are two sides to the art of embroidery. It may be considered as a pictorial art in which the material used serves merely as a surface or ground to be entirely covered with work, like the canvas of a picture. It may also be considered as a decorative art by means of which a woven stuff is ornamented with borders and designs more or less elaborate, but the textile used not playing so entirely subordinate a part as in the former case. The more important and pictorial side is usually left in the hands of professional workers of experience and skill, but the decorative and more popular work is quite within the scope of amateurs, and is indeed often more beautiful as mere ornament, though its intellectual value may not be so great."

The beginning of the nineteenth century saw the craze for Berlin woolwork take over. Berlin woolwork was a form of needlepoint (tent stitch or cross stitch usually) using wools imported from Germany. It became so popular that by 1840, Berlin woolwork was practically the only form of embroidery pattern produced; a contemporary book, *The Illuminated Book of Needlework*, stated, "Embroidery, or as it is now commonly called, Berlin woolwork …". It featured realistic three-dimensional designs, often after popular engravings such as those by Landseer. Spaniels (see Figure 4) were extremely popular since they were the pets of the young Queen Victoria.

Berlin woolwork required no design skill, since the canvas was marked for the worker, and little embroidery skill. It was more like following a paint-by-numbers kit than painting a picture. As Alexander Koch memorably wrote in *Moderne Stickereien (Modern Embroidery)*, a book published in 1908, "No art-work so much practiced by our women so little understands their aesthetic nature as embroidery. The careful observer must be saddened as an enormous amount of love and diligence is wasted for months on inexpressibly banal and tasteless cushions and doilies. … The new art form obtains its most beautiful effects via simplicity, unlike the often incomprehensible needle-paintings with their unbelievably complicated eye- and nerve-killing technology."

The three-dimensional pictorial effects often aimed at with Berlin woolwork fell directly under the purview of *direct imitation of nature*, so it was anathema to Mr. Henry Cole. Fortunately, during the 1850s, when Henry Cole was trying to reform design in Britain, a young, wealthy man with artistic tendencies was becoming very interested in medieval art, including embroidery. His name was William Morris.

Figure 4. Hand-painted Berlin woolwork pattern by Louis Gluer, a German designer.

Chapter 2

Morris Embroideries

William Morris is one of those towering figures that the Victorian age specialized in (see Figure 5). He was a genius in pattern design, a poet and writer of repute, a book designer, a weaver and dyer, an astute businessman, decorator, illustrator, preservationist, and oh yes, a political organizer. Anything he did, he did well and did thoroughly. For example, he wanted to read some Icelandic sagas that hadn't been translated into English, so he learned Old Norse and translated them himself.

Morris grew up in a wealthy family in East London. He went to Marlborough College and then Oxford. Morris first became interested in embroidery around 1856, according to his wife Jane. He fell in love with medieval art while articled (similar to an apprenticeship) to the Gothic Revival architect G.E. Street. In medieval times, embroidery was considered one of the highest forms of art, along with stained glass. (At that time, men who wanted to become architects paid a practitioner to be taught the profession. Before 1832, there were only two universities in England, Oxford and Cambridge, and neither thought architecture was worthy of university study. Anyway, Morris left his articles because he wanted to be a painter.)

As with every other craft he was interested in, William Morris set about teaching himself to embroider and discovering how medieval embroideries were created. Jane Morris told Morris's biographer that "We studied old pieces and by unpicking, etc., we learnt much—but it was uphill work, fascinating, but only carried through by his enormous perseverance." Henry James wrote in 1869 about watching Morris embroider, aided by his wife and children, who were then eight and seven years old. (As we shall see, May, the seven year old, grew up to be not only the director of the embroidery department at Morris & Co. at age twenty-three, but a towering figure in the world of needlework.) Henry James to his sister Alice: "Morris's poetry, you see, is only his sub-trade. To begin with, he is a manufacturer of stained glass windows, tiles, ecclesiastical and medieval tapestry, altar-cloths, and

Figure 5. William Morris, author's own photo, c. 1872.

in fine everything quaint, archaic, pre-Raphaelite and I may add, exquisite. Of course his business is small and may be carried on in his house: the things he makes are so handsome, rich, and expensive (besides being articles of the very last luxury) that his fabrique can't be on a very large scale. But everything he has and does is superb and beautiful. But more curious than anything is himself. He designs with his own head and hands all the figures and patterns used in his glass and tapestry, and furthermore works the latter, stitch by stitch, with his own fingers aided by those of his wife and little girls."

Figure 6. *Penelope*, worked by Bessie Burden, c. 1860 (embroidery on serge), Kelmscott Manor, Oxfordshire, UK. *Courtesy Bridgeman Art Library.*

A large and ambitious set of early embroideries by Morris, sadly not completed, were intended to adorn the dining room at Red House, which was to be his marital home. They were designed to replicate the kind of tapestry that would be used in an English medieval interior, so mostly crewels were used to create them, not silk. Each piece was embroidered on linen, then cut out and appliquéd to panels of wool, which was also to be embroidered. There were supposed to be twelve large female figures, loosely based on Chaucer's *Legend of Good Women* (except the surviving pieces aren't heroines from that work, so maybe Morris just decided to honor different women). These pieces were by Jane, with help from her sister Elizabeth (Bessie) Burden. Figure 6 shows Penelope from the set.

Morris, Marshall, Faulkner & Co. was founded at a fortunate time. The Church of England was worried about declining church attendance in the 1840s and 1850s, so embarked on a church-building and remodeling frenzy. Morris & Co. received many commissions for ecclesiastical work, especially in stained glass and embroidery. Embroidery was an important part of the Morris business from the beginning. During the later 1860s, the church business lessened, so Morris concentrated on domestic commissions. (And sometimes they lost commissions deliberately. Morris's business manager Warrington Taylor lost a bid for church decoration by writing on the estimate: "To providing a silk and gold altar cloth: 'Note—In consideration of the fact that the above item is wholly unnecessary and inexcusable at a time when thousands of poor people in this so-called Christian country are in want of food—additional charge to that set forth, ten pounds'." Morris laughed and said he was glad to make Taylor into a socialist.)

At first, family members of the company principals did the embroidery: Jane and Bessie, Georgiana Burne-Jones, and Kate and Lucy Faulkner. When the business expanded, the firm took on workers, who were managed by Jane and Bessie. One of the best known embroiderers who worked freelance for Morris was Catherine Holiday, wife of the painter Henry Holiday. Morris encouraged the embroiderers to contribute to the design of the work, but he seems to have realized the importance of branding, of the Morris look, very early. Morris wallpapers, chintzes, embroideries and so on all harmonized beautifully, and decorating and books on taste recognized the superiority of "Morrisian" designs.

Morris & Co. made some large, very expensive embroidered pieces, but also sold transfers or kits for smaller items: table squares, fire screens, work bags, cushion covers, and so on. The kits were available as: a canvas with just a line drawing; a colored design on the canvas, including the threads to stitch; the painted canvas and threads with samples of stitching worked on the edge; or the design stitched and only the background left to do.

In the 1870s, Morris concentrated on designing repeated patterns for fabric and wallpaper, so it's not surprising that his embroidery designs tend to be repeating patterns. Figure 7 shows the *Artichoke* hanging, which was designed by Morris for the dining room of Smeaton Manor in 1877, which was then worked by the owner. Ada Phoebe Godman, the chatelaine of Smeaton Manor, spent countless hours embroidering a set of these panels, in crewel wool on linen, to cover the walls of her dining room. *Artichoke* was one of the earliest kits sold by Morris & Co.

Figure 8. Honeysuckle pattern by William Morris. *Handbook of Embroidery*.

The *Honeysuckle* embroidery design in Figure 8, from the *Royal School of Art Needlework* handbook, was originally designed by Morris c. 1876 for Jane Morris to do while reclining on her sofa. (She suffered from ill health.) *Honeysuckle* was May Morris's favorite design—she considered it "the most truly Morrisian" of her father's works.

Figure 9 is probably a later pattern of Morris's, after he started creating squared off designs. It also might possibly be by Henry Dearle. A later non-repeating design by Morris, *The Flowerpot* (see Figure 10), is adapted from seventeenth-century Italian lace in the Victoria and Albert Museum.

William Morris died at the relatively young age of 62, probably of diabetes. His doctor famously attributed his death to "simply being William Morris, and having done more work than most ten men."

Figure 7. Artichoke panel by William Morris. Planet Art CD, *William Morris: Selected Works.*

May Morris (see Figure 11) took over the embroidery department of Morris & Co. at the age of twenty-three in 1885. Her father had confidence in her abilities, because the embroidery department was one of the most important in the Firm. Mary Lobb, who had a romantic relationship with May later in life, wrote to the director of the Victoria and Albert Museum after May's death, "You see William Morris could design embroideries but he could not embroider [...] Mrs. Morris could embroider but couldn't design, Miss Morris could and did both design as well as William Morris and embroider as well as any one possibly could and her color arrangements were approachable and original [...] This is where Miss Morris excelled and that is what so few grasp and appreciate."

May was known for her use of color, which was far less subdued than Morris's. She wrote, "... color cannot be too bright in itself; if it appears so, it is the skill of the craftsman that is at fault. It will be noted in a fine piece of work that far from blazing with color in a way to disturb the eye, its general effect is that of a subdued glow; and yet, on considering the different shades of the colors used, they are found to be in themselves of the brightest the dyer can produce. Thus I have seen in an old Persian rug light and dark blue flowers and orange leaves outlined with turquoise blue on a strong red ground, a combination that sounds daring, and yet nothing could be more peaceful in tone than the beautiful and complicated groups of colors here displayed. Harmony, then, produces this repose, which is demanded instinctively, purity and crispness being further obtained by the quality of the colors used." (*Arts and Crafts Essays*, 1903.)

Figure 9. A Morris & Co. silk embroidered panel decorated with four flowerheads inside a border of scrolling leaf. *Courtesy Woolley and Wallis.*

Figure 10. *The Flowerpot* by William Morris. *The Studio Volume 12.*

Figure 11. May Morris pictured in 1909. *Bain News Service, Library of Congress.*

Figure 12. Christening mittens designed by Charles Ricketts and executed by May Morris, silks on linen. Worked for the christening of Daniel Sturge Moore, c. 1900. *Courtesy V&A Images/Victoria and Albert Museum.*

Figure 14. Curtain by May Morris. *Modern Decorative Art in England.*

One example of May's beautiful use of color is Figure 12, a pair of christening mittens designed by Charles Ricketts and embroidered by May. The reds and pinks are bright but not too overpowering paired with the cooler greens and blues. Charles Ricketts also designed a pair of bishop's Easter gloves worked by May with gold ears of wheat, shown in Figure 13. (I don't know; maybe he just liked gloves.)

In addition to her use of brighter colors, May's work is characterized by more humble British native plants than her father's. Morris used the classical acanthus leaves heavily, as did Dearle; May generally didn't. But like her father, May used birds extensively in her designs, as well as embroidered mottoes. The curtain design in Figure 14 is similar to the bed cover for her father's bedroom at Kelmscott Manor, which was worked by herself, Lily Yeats, and others. It's a looser, freer netted design than was used on her father's work, a feeling which also comes across in the embroidered sleeve illustrated in Figure 15.

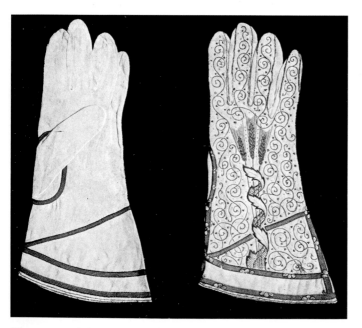

Figure 13. Bishop's gloves designed by Charles Ricketts and executed by May Morris. *The Art Journal Volume 69.*

Figure 15. Embroidered sleeve, yes just a sleeve, by May Morris. *The Magazine of Fine Arts Volume 1.*

Figure 16 shows a design of pomegranates and carnations I am attributing to May on the basis of the colors used. Figure 17 shows a close up of the design. Carnations or pinks also show up in the border of a table square by Morris & Co. (see Figure 18). Figures 19 and 20 show two color variants of another floral design.

Figure 17. Close up of pomegranates. *Courtesy Woolley and Wallis*.

Figure 18. An embroidered silk panel, worked with a border of scrolling carnations. *Courtesy Woolley and Wallis*.

Figure 16. Morris & Co. silk embroidery, worked with a spray of pomegranates on a cream embroidered ground. *Courtesy Woolley and Wallis*.

Figure 19. Silk panel by May Morris. *Courtesy Lyon & Turnbull.*

Figure 21 is an interesting piece, possibly by May or by Dearle. It was probably sold as a kit for a table square and then someone had it made, possibly later, into a mirror frame. It was worked by Emily Cannon.

An embroidered cushion in white velvet, with doves, is shown in Figure 22. The piece was shown at the Arts and Crafts Exhibition in 1906. *The Studio* praised the "… quite unusual degree of beauty in its designing. It is, frankly, a cushion made for the sake of its design and for effectiveness. It could never come into the ordinary rough service which the useful cushions of a room get, for the pattern is carried out on an almost white surface of plush."

When May managed the Morris embroidery department, her workrooms were in Kelmscott House, the Morris family home in Hammersmith, London. There, workers such as Lily Yeats (who didn't like May and who referred to her as "the Gorgon" and a "she-cat" in her scrapbook) and Mary de Morgan (the fairy tale author and sister of potter William) stitched away.

Figure 21. An Arts and Crafts mahogany and embroidery framed mirror, the borders worked by Emily Cannon with flowering scroll foliage, circa 1920. *Courtesy Dreweatt Neate Fine Art.*

Figure 20. This table cover by May Morris was embroidered circa 1890 and was made for the Barr-Smith residence in Adelaide, Australia. *Photo by Simone Chaves Kullberg.*

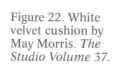

Figure 22. White velvet cushion by May Morris. *The Studio Volume 37.*

(Lily Yeats, the poet and artist's sister, worked as an embroiderer to make ends meet, despite chronic illness. Figure 23 shows a work by Lily c. 1900. W.B. and Jack lived on their sisters' meager earnings. Lily wrote, "I worked in the Morris dining room in Kelmscott House—a beautiful room with three large portraits of Mrs. Morris by Rossetti and a drawing called 'Pomona.' At the end of the room was a large window looking into the garden and on the wall facing the fireplace was a Persian carpet hanging on the wall. Across the window was a plain oak unpolished and unstained table at which I worked. May very seldom did any work, just used to look at mine." Scrapbook of Lily Yeats, quoted in *The Yeats Sisters and the Cuala* by Gifford Lewis.)

May Morris lived at Kelmscott Manor in her later years; she also worked tirelessly to improve education in regards to needlework, publishing many articles and a number of books on the subject.

Figure 23. *Peonies and Plums*, a silk embroidered cushion cover by Lily Yeats, signed. This piece belonged to her first cousin, Dr. Rupert Gordon, and was made in Dublin c. 1903. *Courtesy Whyte's.*

Henry Dearle

John Henry Dearle (1860-1932) began his career as an assistant in Morris & Co.'s shop in Oxford Street in 1878. He also studied design. William Morris was working on setting up a loom for tapestry at this time, and recognizing Dearle's talent, made him his tapestry assistant. As Morris became more interested in other things, like politics and writing, Dearle rose through the ranks of the company designing stained glass, wallpapers, carpets, and fabrics, as well as tapestries and embroidery. By 1890, Dearle was chief designer at Morris & Co.

Dearle's design style is closer to William Morris's than May's, but even so it can be difficult to know who designed what. Most of the output of Morris & Co. was sold without a designer's name, unless it was Morris's of course. And the "Morrisian" house style was followed.

However, it is known that the screen in Figures 24 and 25, which were very popular and available in several styles, were designed by Dearle in the mid-1880s. The embroidered panels are the *Parrot Tulip*, *Large Horned Poppy*, and *Anemone* designs. These screens were available as kits or made up at the Morris & Co. workrooms. An identical screen showing two of these panels was illustrated in Morris & Co.'s *Embroidery Work* catalogue published about 1910, priced at £17 10s. (About $2500 today—I'll take two.) This particular screen was owned by Barbara Morris, who worked at the Victoria and Albert Museum and wrote books about Victorian embroidery. She believed that May Morris designed the panel on the right.

Figure 24. A Morris & Co. three fold embroidered screen, three rectangular panels of various embroidered floral designs, designed by John Henry Dearle circa 1885-1890. *Courtesy Woolley and Wallis.*

Figure 25. Detail of *Parrot Tulip* design in Morris & Co. screen. *Courtesy Woolley and Wallis.*

Figure 26 shows a Morris & Co. silk embroidered panel, by Helen, Lady Lucas Tooth, the design attributed to John Henry Dearle. The silk ground fabric is the *Oak* pattern favored by both Dearle and May Morris for their richer, more luxurious hangings. The piece is embroidered with peony stems and acanthus leaves. Lady Lucas Tooth embroidered a set of six Dearle designs between 1919 and 1923, which are now in the William Morris Gallery, Walthamstow, east London (Morris's childhood home). Helen, Lady Lucas Tooth, was the wife of Sir Robert Lucas Tooth, an Australian brewer who eventually settled in England permanently.

Figure 26. A Morris & Co. silk embroidered panel, by Helen, Lady Lucas Tooth; the printed *Oak* silk ground embroidered with peony stems and acanthus leaves. *Courtesy Woolley and Wallis.*

Next is a large Morris & Co. silk embroidery panel, with green velvet border (see Figures 27 and 28). The use of grapes is somewhat unusual, though Morris had earlier put out an embroidery design with a grape tree probably done by Philip Webb. A very similar grapevine motif by Dearle was executed in Arras tapestry.

Figure 28. Detail of Morris & Co. silk embroidery panel. *Courtesy Woolley and Wallis.*

Figure 27. A large Morris & Co. silk embroidery panel with green velvet border. *Courtesy Woolley and Wallis.*

The last two designs are attributed to Dearle. This work (Figure 29) is said to be by William Morris in *Modern Decorative Art in England* (1922) but it's said to be by Dearle in *The Studio Year-Book* of 1906. But then work by Dearle usually was attributed to Morris. May liked to use tulips in her designs, as in the *Apple Tree* embroidery. Figure 30 may be by May or by Dearle.

Following Morris's death in 1896, Dearle was appointed art director of the firm. Dearle carried on with Morris & Co. until his own death in 1932; his designs were pleasant, but decorative arts continued to evolve and the firm did not. The company was eventually put in receivership at the outbreak of World War II.

Figure 30. A Morris & Co. silk embroidered panel, decorated with pink tulip flowers. *Courtesy Woolley and Wallis.*

Figure 29. Panel by Morris & Co. *Modern Decorative Art in England.*

Chapter 3

Art Needlework

Unlike the counted-thread technique of Berlin woolwork, the new needlework popularized by Morris emphasized delicate shading using satin, long-and-short, and other stitches on conventionalized natural designs. A number of embroidery societies were founded to improve the design and standard of embroidery, to give employment to the many women of gentle birth who needed employment, and of course to sell silk. The first and most famous of these societies is the Royal School of Art Needlework (RSAN) in 1872, which still exists today (now known as the Royal School of Needlework).

Founded by two ladies, Lady Marian Alford (see Figure 31) and Miss Helen Welby, and patronized by a daughter of Queen Victoria, the Royal School of Art Needlework had the mission of "supplying suitable employment for gentlewomen and restoring ornamental needlework to the high place it once held among the decorative arts." It commissioned designs from many well-known artists, including Morris, Edward Burne-Jones, Selwyn Image, and Walter Crane. Later, May Morris was heavily involved with the school and Bessie Burden was chief technical instructor. As well as selling finished embroideries specially designed for it, the school repaired antique textiles and sold printed fabrics designed to be worked at home by amateurs. They also copied old designs.

By 1876, the RSAN boasted 110 workers and 20 staff teachers. There were six work departments: the general workroom, the prepared work department (for items to be sold with the embroidery done), pricking and pouncing (methods of applying designs to fabric), appliqué and goldwork, upholstery, and the artistic room, where the highest-quality designs were done. There were four tiers of pay for embroiderers, based on how fast and accurate a worker was: 10d (pence) an hour, 9d, 7.5d, and 6d. (These work out to £17.80, £16.10, £13.40 and £10.70 in 2012 using an average earnings calculator, or $27 an hour on down. Not bad.)

Embroidery lessons were £5 for 9 of 5 hours each. That was steep and a price a working-class girl wouldn't have been able to pay; this makes it clear that the school was for impoverished gentlewomen. The work was needed: the 1881 census indicated that women in England outnumbered men by 695,000. A gentlewoman needed a job that afforded her dignity in accordance with her standing in society, yet gentlewomen were not given the education that would enable them to take up professional work, even assuming such were open to them. Art work was one answer.

Designing, however, was not the aim at the school. Lady Marian Alford gave an address in 1875 in which she stated, "I would impress on all, workers and superintendents too, that nothing should be left to the imagination of the stitcher, that each must copy humbly and faithfully the design which should always be before her." This is of course antithetical to the ideal of art in which it is designed and created by a single person. The RSAN produced a number of spectacular works of embroidery, and it raised the standard of workmanship a great deal, but artistically, much of the RSAN's output was mediocre. The RSAN relied on copying of antique work and of designs supplied to it by artists. This did raise the profile of embroidery, since after all *men* were designing for it. The RSAN also had a Committee of Taste with artists such as Lord Leighton, Edward Poynter, Burne-Jones, and Val Prinsep on it.

J.D. Sedding, in his essay "Design" (1903) wrote "The honor of the British nation, the credit of Royalty, are, in a manner, staked upon the success of our 'Schools of Needlework.' And yet, in spite of all these favoring circumstances, we get no nearer to the old work that first mocked us to emulation in regard to power of initiative and human interest.

"Truth and gallantry prompt me to add, it is not in stitchery but in design that we lag behind the old. Fair English hands can copy every trick of ancient artistry: finger-skill was never defter, will was never more ardent to do fine things, than now. Yet our work hangs fire. It fails in design. Why?

"Mark this, however: that whereas the design of old needlework is based upon enthusiasm for birds, flowers, and animal life, the design of modern needlework has its origin in enthusiasm for antique art."

Figure 32. Design for chair back embroidery by George Aitchison. *Handbook of Embroidery*.

Figure 33. Design for chair back embroidery by William Morris. *Handbook of Embroidery*.

By 1880, art needlework had become all the rage. Elizabeth Glaister wrote in *Needlework* (1880): "A great deal of haze still hangs over this question of Art Needlework in the mind of that large section of womankind which uses the needle for pleasure and beauty, rather than for use and of necessity. Many people think that no more is needed than to work in crewels on crash [a type of linen] instead of, as formerly, in Berlin wool on canvas. Others, that if work be in 'dowdy' colors and rather badly done it may pass under the sacred name of Art. Others again show a blind and touching faith in South Kensington, and maintain that 'Art Needlework' is only to be had there; while a more enterprising friend replies that most of the shops have it now, though you cannot get it at the 'Stores', [The Army & Navy Co-operative Society] and she buys hers at Whiteley's. [Whiteley's was London's first department store, known as the Universal Provider.] All would say that it is a modern invention, much in fashion just now, and therefore they must by no means neglect it."

Figure 31. Lady Marian Alford. *Courtesy British Library*.

W. G. Paulson Townsend, Design Master at the school, modestly stated in his book *Embroidery, Or the Craft of the Needle* (1899), "Excellent needlework was produced in England in the seventeenth century, and some of the best examples in crewel work have been copied by the Royal School of Art Needlework; in fact, the revival of this kind of embroidery is entirely due to the efforts put forward by the School, where for many years they have been engaged in making hangings, curtains, valances, bedspreads, and furniture covering, using the old crewel-work designs." Figures 32 and 33 show designs for chair backs available from the RSAN and Figure 34 shows a design of birds and acanthus leaves worked by RSAN.

Figure 34. Circa 1915-1920 silk panel of stylized birds amongst flora and foliage by the Royal School of Art Needlework. *Courtesy Hill House Antiques*.

The RSAN became well known in America when they sent a stand of goods to the Philadelphia Centennial Exposition, where they impressed a lady called Candace Wheeler, who you'll meet later. *Harper's Bazar* began publishing needlework designs in America from the RSAN in the 1880s (see Figures 35 and 36).

The flowers pictured in art needlework tend to be "aesthetic" flowers: sunflowers (see Figure 37), lilies, irises, conventionalized daisies, and so on. Swans, doves, and peacocks were popular designs; as for fruit, pomegranates, apples, and grapes were common fruit designs. Figure 38 shows a satirical cartoon from *Punch*. The flowers on the lady's dress are so realistic, the bee and others think they're real. On the left it says, "Patterns Morris & Co."; on the right is a reference to Helbronner, called in the magazine *Household Words* a "high-class fancywork shop" located in Regent Street.

Figure 35. Design for embroidery by the Royal School of Art Needlework. *Harper's Bazar, May 24, 1881.*

Figure 37. Peacock green plush velvet panel embroidered with sunflowers in old gold, natural, browns, and green wool with silk highlights. *Courtesy Meg Andrews.*

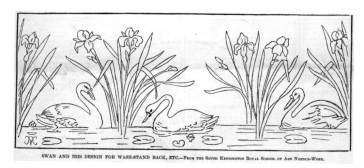

SWAN AND IRIS DESIGN FOR WASH-STAND BACK, ETC.—FROM THE SOUTH KENSINGTON ROYAL SCHOOL OF ART NEEDLE-WORK.

Figure 36. Design for embroidery by the Royal School of Art Needlework. *Harper's Bazar, May 24, 1881.*

Figure 38. "Sweet Little Buttercup; Or, Art Embroidery 1879," by Linley Sambourne. "Buttercup" is a reference to *HMS Pinafore* by Gilbert and Sullivan. The lady is standing on something from the "School of Art Embroidery," and there are patterns from Morris & Co. and Helbronner. *Punch*, June 14, 1879.

Edward Burne-Jones

Edward Burne-Jones (1833–1898) was of course a Pre-Raphaelite artist and best friend of William Morris, but he was also an important part of Morris & Co. He designed stained glass, tiles, jewelry, tapestries, and illustrated books. He began designing figures for embroidery very early in his career, a set of works for the Red House. He also designed another large set of embroideries in 1874 to decorate the dining room of another Philip Webb-designed house called Rounton Grange. They were based on Chaucer's *The Romaunt of the Rose*; in the 1880s and '90s Burne-Jones adapted the designs for paintings. Burne-Jones's work seems to have been very flexible, in that work designed for embroidery could be adapted for paintings, and work designed for stained glass could be adapted for embroidery. Figure 39 is *Faith*, a silk embroidered panel worked by N. Victoria Wade. Burne-Jones's original design was for a stained glass window installed at Christ Church Cathedral, Oxford, in 1870–71.

Figure 40 shows *Pomona*, a gigantic work of embroidery (ten feet high!), an adaptation of a tapestry design that was executed by RSAN. The figure was embroidered, while the face and hands were painted by Burne-Jones. The background was designed by William Morris. The grapes on the border are padded to give them extra emphasis.

It was exhibited by Morris & Co. at the World's Columbia Exposition in Chicago in 1893. Not everyone was a fan. W.G. Paulson Townsend wrote of it in *Embroidery or the Craft of the Needle*, "… in the writer's opinion, the scrolls are too large in relation to the figure." Lady Marian Alford, the founder of RSAN, wrote about Morris's "repetitions of large vegetable forms, which remind us sometimes of a kitchen-garden in a tornado." (*Needlework as Art*, 1888) Ouch.

Figure 40. *Pomona*, designed by Edward Burne-Jones and William Morris, worked by the Royal School of Art Needlework. *Embroidery: Or, the Craft of the Needle.*

Figure 39. *Faith*, a silk embroidered panel, worked by N. Victoria Wade, c. 1890. *Courtesy Woolley and Wallis.*

Edward Burne-Jones also designed embroidery for RSAN. Figure 41 appears in *Handbook of Embroidery* by L. Higgin (1880); its description states it should be "worked in outline on neutral-tinted hand-woven linen in brown crewel."

Figure 42 is a book cover exhibited in 1904. This was embroidered by Aglaia Coronio, the younger sister of Constantine Ionides and the daughter of Alexander Ionides, who were fabulously rich art patrons. Aglaia was a confidante of William Morris's and a cousin of Burne-Jones's model and lover Maria Zambaco. Aglaia also helped Burne-Jones in his studio. Lady Burne-Jones wrote in 1906, "Her perfect taste helped him a hundred times by finding fabrics and arranging dresses for models."

Figure 41. Design for crewel embroidery by Edward Burne-Jones. *Handbook of Embroidery*.

Figure 42. Book cover designed by Edward Burne-Jones; worked by Aglaia Coronio. *The Studio Volume 30*.

Selwyn Image

Selwyn Image (1849-1930) was a clergyman, designer, and poet. He relinquished his holy orders in 1880 when he decided to concentrate on art. He cofounded the Century Guild and edited the guild's magazine, *The Hobby Horse*. *The Hobby Horse* published essays by May Morris about embroidery, among other things like pictures by Charles Ricketts. Selwyn Image lectured about modern art, later becoming Slade Professor of Fine Arts at Oxford. A significant figure in decadent London, he was friendly with Oscar Wilde. After Wilde's arrest, Image urged his friend Stewart Headlam, with whom he formed the Anti-Puritan League in protest, to bail Wilde from prison, which Headlam did.

While he was still Reverend Image, in 1879, he designed a series of Roman goddess designs for the RSAN (see Figures 43 and 44). Figure 45 shows a completed screen. These look very similar to the goddesses, muses, and so on produced by Burne-Jones, Walter Crane, Ellen Welby, and others. Classical references demonstrated one's taste and education in the Victorian age. Oscar Wilde's magazine *Woman's World* was referring to these figures when author E.T. Masters wrote, "Very truly pleasing, on the other hand, are the figures of heathen goddesses and classical heroines that are intended for the panels of screens, and which are carried out solely in fine thread of a soft brown color, so that when finished they resemble sepia drawings or etchings more than ordinary needlework. Special care must be taken in outlining the features of the faces to avoid the appearance of a caricature. It is really wonderful how slight a deviation from the outline will spoil the expression of the faces in embroidery of this sort. The folds of drapery, plumage of birds, foliage, and such details require the stitches to be massed, but otherwise the work is entirely carried out in outline stitch. Venus, Juno, Hygeia, Minerva, Proserpine, are a few only of the graceful female figures that are prepared for embroidery in this style."

Figure 43. Design for embroidered screen by Selwyn Image. *Handbook of Embroidery*.

Figure 44. Design for embroidered screen by Selwyn Image. *Handbook of Embroidery*.

Figure 45. An Aesthetic Movement four-fold screen worked in brown wool with goddesses labeled Minerva, Juno, Prosephone, and Venus, the reverse with flowers, in a walnut frame. *Courtesy Dreweatt Neate Fine Art.*

Flowers are not that hard to represent in needlework, as long as the design is conventional, of course. What about representing the human form? You can't conventionalize a human being and make it recognizable, can you? Go carefully, say all the designers. It is extremely difficult to render a human form with beauty via embroidery, which is probably why human figures are generally the most carefully done embroideries you can find. There is almost none of it to be found in American Arts and Crafts, which makes sense considering that most of it was done via kit form.

Lewis F. Day, the designer and critic, wrote, "Needlework, like any other decorative craft, demands treatment in the design, and the human figure submits less humbly to the necessary modification than other forms of life. Animals, for instance, lend themselves more readily to it, and so do birds; fur and feathers are obviously translatable into stitches. Leaves and flowers accommodate themselves perhaps better still; but each is best when it is only the motive, not the model, of design. If only, then, on account of the greater difficulty in treating it, the figure is not the form of design most likely to do credit to the needle, and it is absurd to argue that, figure work being the noblest form of design, therefore the noblest form of embroidery must include it. The embroidress entirely in sympathy with her materials will not want telling that the needle lends itself better to forms less fixed in their proportions than the human figure ..." (*Art in Needlework*, 1907.)

Figure A shows a Burne-Jones design in silk. It's well-done and a lovely image, but I'm not very happy about the way the flesh and the fabric are just about the same tone and texture. Another figural piece with embroidered skin is Figure B, a girl with a dove, which I find more appealing (or maybe it's just that the colors have faded differently? It's hard to tell now).

Figure A. Close up of *Faith*, a silk embroidered panel, worked by N. Victoria Wade, c. 1890. *Courtesy Woolley and Wallis.*

Figure B. Embroidered panel in colored silks, probably Scottish, c. 1900. *Courtesy of Lyon & Turnbull.*

The best figural designs, in my view, were done by Ann Macbeth, the great Glasgow designer. Her ladies aren't realistic, but they are lovely and recognizably human (see Figure C). She wrote in *Educational Needlecraft*, "The treatment of the human figure in embroidery has always been the highest and most difficult achievement of the craft, and the methods of working employed are a somewhat vexed question. [...] If the effect of painting is desired, paint is the medium which most quickly arrives at that effect. Embroidery has characteristics so exclusively and beautifully its own that it should be the aim of its designer to make use of these to their fullest extent, without straining the material beyond the limits to which its texture confines it. Therefore it is not needful to treat flesh tints in difficult and intricate shading of tone. Better it is to treat the face, for instance, by means of simple and dignified outlines in suitable neutral tint."

What about mixing paint and embroidery, as has been done in Figure D, a rather lovely rendering of Pandora, executed at the Royal School of Art Needlework? Lewis F. Day is firmly against it. "... the mixture of painting and embroidery is not to be endured; and it is a poor-spirited embroidress who will thus confess her weakness and call on painting to help her out. It does not even do that, it fails absolutely to produce the desired effect. The painting quarrels with the stitching, and there is after all no semblance of that unity which is the very essence of picture."

Figure C. *The Bride* by Ann Macbeth, *Educational Needlecraft.*

Figure D. Embroidered panel, *Pandora Opening Her Box,* circa 1910, watercolor detail, labeled verso for Royal School of Art Needlework. *Courtesy Tennants Auctioneers.*

Offlow Scattergood is a name you don't run into that often. *The Art Journal* wrote that she was "a young lady whose work, probably owing to her singular name, has been criticized as that of a man in more than one newspaper." Good old Offlow won a gold medal and a scholarship in embroidery during the 1898 National Competition of Schools of Art. She was a student at Birmingham School of Art. Figure E shows her prizewinning designs; at least one of the panels still exists today (see Figure F). Offlow exhibited regularly at the Royal Society of Artists, Birmingham, but sadly died young in 1910.

Figure E. Embroidery designs by Offlow Scattergood. *The Studio Volume 14.*

Figure F. An embroidered picture designed and executed by Offlow Scattergood, of a maiden with sea birds on the shore, titled below "Across the strand far up the land /The fierce wild waters swept," named in ink to upper stretcher labeled "Birmingham Municipal." *Courtesy Dreweatt Neate Fine Art.*

Walter Crane

Walter Crane (1845–1915) was, like his friend William Morris, another of those versatile Victorian giants in the arts. He's mostly known today as an artist and children's book illustrator, but he was active in most branches of the decorative arts, the Arts and Crafts Exhibition Society, and the socialist movement. He also wrote a number of books on design. He designed a great deal of embroidery; some specifically for embroidery and some adapted from or into designs for wallpaper or other things. Figure 46 shows a screen designed by Crane and made by the RSAN, which was shown at the 1876 Philadelphia Centennial Exposition.

Another item made by the RSAN to Crane's design is shown in Figure 47, a screen with embodiments of the senses of sight, smell, hearing, and taste.

Figure 46. Screen designed by Walter Crane and executed by the Royal School of Art Needlework. *The Masterpieces of the Centennial International Exhibition Illustrated, Volume 2.*

Figure 47. Screen designed by Walter Crane and worked by the Royal School of Art Needlework. *Embroidery: Or, the Craft of the Needle.*

Figure 48 is a portière made by Mrs. Crane, which was shown at the 1899 Arts and Crafts Exhibition. *The Studio* noted that it was "worthy to rank beside any of the best of Mr. Crane's artistic achievements. The portière, designed for his own house, was executed in silks, cotton, and gold and silver thread on blue linen by Mrs. Crane. It is divided horizontally into three unequal parts. The uppermost represents 'Luna'; in the middle is a figure of Mother Earth standing with outstretched hands and surrounded by a circular band charged with the signs of the Zodiac; and below is the chariot of the Sun. The greater part is worked in outline, the three principal figures and the sun's horse comprising practically everything that is carried out in solid embroidery."

Figure 49 is a work done by an unknown lady and is incomplete. *Swan, Rush and Iris* was one of Crane's earliest wallpaper designs in 1875. Jeffrey & Co. then produced a similar wallpaper set with frieze, field, and dado, incorporating irises, rushes, and kingfishers. The swans were in the dado. I'm not sure when this design was adapted for embroidery, probably c. 1880. (I like unfinished embroidery. It's good to know some ladies 130 years ago didn't have a long attention span either.)

Figure 49. *Swan, Rush and Iris* embroidery, silk on wool. *Courtesy Karen Euler.*

Figure 48. Portière designed by Walter Crane and made by Mrs. Crane. *The Studio Volume 18.*

Leek Embroidery Society

Other schools and societies were also affiliated with the RSAN. The most important one was founded in 1879 in Staffordshire. The Leek Embroidery Society was established by Elizabeth Wardle, a skilled embroiderer.

Her husband Thomas Wardle was born in Macclesfield, Cheshire, a center of the English silk industry. He started at his father's silk dyeing firm, then began in his own company in Leek, Staffordshire (see Figure 50). The water of the nearby Churnet River was considered to be very good for dyeing purposes.

Figure 50. Thomas Wardle advertisement from Great International Fisheries Exhibition catalog, 1883.

Wardle was interested in chemistry from a young age. He disliked the aniline (chemical) dyes then becoming popular in the industry, as did William Morris. Elizabeth's brother George Wardle (coincidentally, Elizabeth had the same married and maiden names) worked at Morris & Co. as a draftsman; he introduced Thomas to William Morris. Wardle and Morris then worked together on creating natural vegetable dyes.

Wardle also experimented with a kind of Indian silk called tasar or tussore. It is a wild silk, but wasn't used in the West because it is a natural deep beige, it was hard to bleach and dye, and it was naturally slubbed, which was considered inferior. (Slubs are soft, thick nubs in silk yarn, now usually considered a beautiful feature of natural silk.) Wardle finally figured out that the tussore fiber was naturally coated with a gum; Wardle dissolved the gum and was able to bleach and dye the silk any color he wanted. This helped revitalize both the deeply depressed Indian silk market and also the English silk manufacturing industry.

Wardle also figured out how to reel the tussore silk into thread for embroidery. Thomas's wife Elizabeth was a skilled embroiderer; she and her friends had worked on large church embroideries for many years before Thomas asked her to experiment with his new silk floss. At the time she was having a mental breakdown after the birth of her fourteenth child at the age of forty-two. (And who can blame her?)

Elizabeth found that the long, lustrous fibers of the tussore silk floss made for a beautiful effect, together with Wardle's subtle dyes. The Leek Embroidery Society was born. Thomas was an astute businessman: a society that exhibited its work would elevate the status of that work, which would in turn create a market for his silk. Leek was both a society that sold the work of its members and a school that created new workers.

Leek embroidery work featured densely packed stitches that displayed the luster of the silk, with subtle color shading. The embroidery was often executed onto woven silk brocade for the ecclesiastical designs and onto hand-blocked silk with a repeat pattern for the domestic designs (see Figure 51). Figure 52 is a close-up of a Leek portière now in Parnham House in Surrey.

Figure 51. A Leek Embroidery Society silk embroidered panel with stylized flowers amid scrolling foliage. *Courtesy Woolley and Wallis.*

Figure 52. Close up of a door curtain made by the Leek Embroidery Society for Parham House in west Sussex, circa 1890. *Photo by Simone Chaves Kullberg.*

Most of the output of the Leek Embroidery Society was ecclesiastical and it's pretty rare now. Figure 53 shows the beautifully embroidered head of a saint on silk damask, attributed to Leek.

Leek also sold kits complete with silk floss for the amateur. Many designs were created by the architect Richard Norman Shaw, but Morris, JD Sedding, and Walter Crane also designed for the society. Leek kits were sold at Liberty & Co., Morris & Co., and Maison Helbronner, as well as its own shop. The work involved embroidering over Wardle's textiles. It did require some skill in interpreting the designs; the work involved using Wardle's subtly shaded silks, often combined with gold threads.

By 1885, Leek had about fifty freelancers who supplied it. There was a large workroom and schoolroom near the Wardles' home. Cushions, antimacassars, curtains, fire screens, and work bags were all sold as finished products.

Figure 53. Silk embroidered saint's head on silk damask with gold metallic thread. *Courtesy Woolley and Wallis.*

More Art Needlework

Ellen Welby, born c. 1852, was a designer and illustrator who worked extensively for many years in different media. I have not been able to document whether she sold designs to RSAN or not. She worked at Minton's Art Pottery Studio and later freelanced, illustrating postcards, children's books, and adult books, including the memorably titled *Heads and What They Tell Us* by W. Pugin Thornton. She often published outline drawings of classical goddesses, muses, senses, and elements. These figures were frequently reproduced in the home art journals of the time (see Figure 54). Figures 55 and 56 shows Air, Figure 57 Ceres, and Figure 58 Poetry.

Figure 54. Design for *Euterpe* by Ellen Welby. *Arts and Crafts Magazine, Volume 2.*

Figure 55. Close up of *Air* by Ellen Welby, c. 1902, a lady reaching for a butterfly in a classical dress; outline embroidered in burnt orange silk; the background densely worked in gold silks on linen. *Courtesy Meg Andrews.*

Figure 56. *Air* by Ellen Welby, c. 1902, the figure reaching for a butterfly, in classical garb, outline embroidered in orange silk, the background densely worked in gold silks on linen. *Courtesy Meg Andrews.*

Figure 57. *Ceres*, designed by Ellen Welby for *The Art Designer*, May 1888, the figure holding a sheaf of grain, foliage, and fruit, draped in a classical dress, outline embroidered in burnt orange silk, the background densely worked in gold silks on linen. *Courtesy Meg Andrews.*

Figure 58. *Poetry*, a silk panel by Ellen Welby in colored silks on linen. *Courtesy Karen Euler.*

If you got sick of classical gods and goddesses, you could embroider some saints. Figures 59 and 60 show two parts of a single piece of ecclesiastical embroidery. The faces are exquisitely worked.

Figure 59. Embroidered angels panel, extremely well executed in fine floss silks outlined with gold wrapped silk on a terracotta silk velvet ground, c. 1880. *Courtesy Meg Andrews.*

Figure 60. Embroidered angels panel, extremely well executed in fine floss silks outlined with gold wrapped silk on a terracotta silk velvet ground, c. 1880. *Courtesy Meg Andrews.*

Alexander Fisher was the enamellist *par excellence*. His work in that medium is jaw-dropping. In his book *The Art of Enameling on Metal*, he wrote, "Even the humblest article of utility deserves to be made beautiful—yes, and ought to be made beautiful; and every student should be made acquainted with the full significance of that fact. He who transforms a common article of daily use into a thing of beauty discharges the same high function as he who is building the greatest temple or painting the finest picture." He did some designing for the RSAN as well; a number of versions of this rose tree motif (Figure 61) exist, worked c. 1904.

Also made around that time is the piece in Figure 62, a set of ten *Moorland Scenes* executed by the RSAN.

Art needlework made embroidery a respected part of the Arts and Crafts Movement, rather than just a fancy-work hobby for ladies with too much time on their hands, but its practitioners weren't considered artists. It was more creative than Berlin woolwork, but it still involved working patterns designed by someone else, like the difference between painting and painting-by-the-numbers.

Figure 61. *Rose Tree*, an embroidered panel from a design by Alexander Fisher, c. 1904, silk floss on silk ground. *Courtesy Woolley and Wallis.*

Figure 62. One of a set of ten embroidered curtains, *Moorland Scenes*, designed by Alexander Fisher. Worked at the Royal School of Art Needlework. *The Art Journal Volume 69.*

Chapter 4

Societies and Guilds

The 1880s saw the mushrooming of societies in England determined to spread the gospel of the new art. Some groups were professional associations and some were primarily philanthropic.

Home Arts and Industries Association

Just as the Great Exhibition of 1851 spurred an interest in better design, so did the Philadelphia Centennial Exposition in 1876, especially in America. One person who was inspired by the exposition was the writer Charles Godfrey Leland. He set up the Public School of Industrial Art to teach handicrafts in Philadelphia. He also published a book in 1880 called *The Minor Arts* that promoted the use of handicrafts to teach a love of art in children and to keep traditional crafts alive in an increasingly mechanized age.

The Cottage Arts Association was founded by Eglantyne Jebb in 1884 to spread these ideas in England and to promote "happy and thrifty home life among the people." Its name was changed to reflect wider activities in 1885 to the Home Arts and Industries Association. One of the most active members of the association was the painter Mary Fraser Tytler. Its first treasurer was the novelist Sir Walter Besant, and some of the artists involved included Leighton, Poynter, and Watts. (Mary Fraser Tytler became Mrs. Watts in 1886. Known then as Mary Seton Watts, she later co-founded the Compton Potters' Arts Guild and the Arts and Crafts Guild in Compton, Surrey.)

The members of the Home Arts and Industries Association believed that traditional crafts helped sustain rural communities and gave personal satisfaction. Also, traditional crafts helped fill leisure hours and kept young people out of mischief The Association funded schools and created opportunities for workers to sell their goods via large and popular exhibitions in London (the Albert Hall, for example) and other cities. (Figure 63 shows an

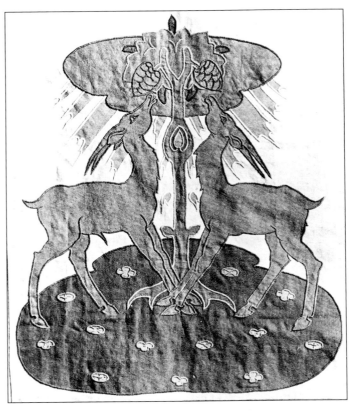

Figure 63. Peasant tapestry designed by Godfrey Blount and shown at the 1900 Home Arts and Industries Exhibition. *The Studio Volume 20.*

embroidery designed by Godfrey Blount from the 1900 Home Arts and Industries Exhibition.)

Of course, both the crafts and the workers were heavily romanticized in these exhibitions. *Every Woman's Encyclopedia* wrote in 1911, "A few hundred years ago England subsisted very largely by her village industries. The weaver, the spinner, the embroiderer were women who sat by their hearthside, for the skillful found it was not difficult to earn money in those days. Then machinery was introduced, and this took the work from the village women's hands, and gave it to the town-dwellers who were ready to work in factories. Not only did this deprive country-people of work, and so of wages, but it often drove them into the towns to less healthy surroundings, keener competition, and a by no means beneficial pressure of work."

The aristocracy from the Princess of Wales on down was involved as patrons, and the Princess even exhibited her own work at times. She also established a school at Sandringham, where girls learned needlework and boys furniture-making, carving, and metalwork.

The association was considered philanthropic. Lady Ishbel Aberdeen gave an address at the Woman's Building, World's Columbian Exposition, Chicago, 1893, called "Encouragement of Home Industries." She said the Home Arts and Industries "has done much good; its aims have been chiefly from the artistic and moral standpoint, rather than from the commercial, though it holds most successful exhibitions and sales annually." Also, the workers were considered amateur. Amateur in those days meant "without professional qualifications," although obviously many of the weavers, knitters, and lacemakers were experts in their fields. And of course, amateur was also a synonym for "female."

Eventually, after classes became better established and the Arts and Crafts movement gained steam, groups associated with the Home Arts and Industries produced extremely high quality work. In metalwork, groups associated with the Home Arts and Industries include the Keswick School of Industrial Arts in the Lake District, the Newlyn Industrial Class in Cornwall, the Yattendon Class in Surrey, the Duchess of Sutherland's Cripples' Guild in Stoke-on-Trent, and the Fivemiletown Class in Ireland. The best known group for embroidery was the Haslemere Peasant Association, which we'll explore below. (Pretty much all of these organizations offered classes in various handicrafts, but most of them are known today for metalwork, not embroidery.)

In the 1880s, all that was in the future. While the Home Arts and Industries was credited with helping to revive interest in handicrafts, it wasn't considered to have advanced the decorative arts. After all, its workers were amateur and often female. Aymer Vallance wrote in the *Magazine of Art*, 1903, "As a consequence of the vogue of arts and crafts it is not unusual for well-disposed but injudicious persons of position in remote country districts, after haven taken, while in London, a desultory course of lessons in wood-carving or repoussé, bent iron or poker work, to inaugurate and direct classes for the same industry in their own neighborhood. They provide the funds for the requisite tools and materials, and they devote a deal of time to teaching their rustic pupils, but it often happens that, beyond the generous motive that prompted them, the undertaking scarcely merits any further recognition. And when, as is their wont, after a while they invite someone, whose name is well known in connection with arts and crafts, to come down and inspect the work produced, and to

deliver an address in support of it, the unfortunate visitor is at his wits' end to discover how to tell the honest truth without inflicting pain, and without seeming to countenance what is pitifully bad from the artist's point of view, and is yet the outcome of the most excellent intentions. And so he cannot be blamed when the conviction is forced upon him that the cause he loves would fare better were it less patronized by benevolent dilettanti, and but for all sorts of incompetent people having found out that there is no surer way to attract the notice of the public than to label oneself a 'craftsman', and one's wares 'decorative art'." (Harsh.)

Designers, architects, and artists increasingly believed that the applied arts should be on an equal footing with fine arts. Clearly, professional men with degrees instead of aristocratic, do-gooder ladies needed to form an association.

The Art Workers' Guild

Architects, designers, and craftsmen were chafing at the narrow view of art promulgated by the Royal Academy (which was founded for architecture, painting, and sculpture). (Holman Hunt wrote to Walter Crane that "as at present constituted the Royal Academy is a perpetual injury to art.") Oil paintings in gilt frames garnered all the attention, while "the lesser arts" got almost none.

The Art Workers' Guild was founded in 1884 to promote the unity of all the arts. It aimed to be "a new Society for promoting more intimate relations between Painters, Sculptors, Architects, and those working in the Arts of Design." By 1885 there were sixty-six members; most were painters or architects, but Walter Crane and Lewis F. Day were both founding members and were both very interested in embroidery.

Another group, the Century Guild, was founded in 1882 by Arthur Heygate Mackmurdo. Its only members were Mackmurdo, Herbert Horne and Selwyn Image. Mackmurdo was an English designer and architect who influenced Voysey and Mackintosh. The Guild doesn't really concern us because its output was small and was mostly furniture and stained glass. It was fairly influential, however, especially because the group published a quarterly magazine called *The Hobby Horse*, which ran until 1894. The Century Guild eventually proved to be too loose of an association to survive; the Art Workers' Guild and the Arts and Crafts Exhibition Society both lasted far longer. In fact, the Art Workers' Guild is still going strong today.

The Art Workers' Guild was not very interested in exhibitions. As a group, it existed more to facilitate the exchange of ideas among its members and to promote cooperation among the various branches of the arts. Some of its members thought that decorative arts exhibitions were important for career success and public support, so therefore another society was needed.

Arts and Crafts Exhibition Society

The Arts and Crafts Exhibition Society was founded in 1887 by prominent artists and designers to promote the decorative arts. (Yes, that is where the movement got its name.) The Arts and Crafts Exhibition Society was the first to display decorative arts as if they were fine arts. And unlike other exhibitions, both designers and makers were named in the exhibition and in the catalog (see Figure 64). This meant that an embroidered picture was displayed as though it was fine art, and the implication was that the skill of the embroiderer and the execution of the design was as important as the designer. In most commercial firms, designers of goods were not named. (Liberty was one of these, as you'll see.) The Society also gave designers a place to publish their theories in the exhibition catalog.

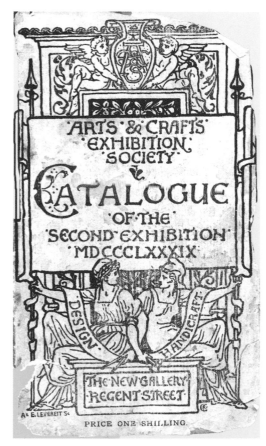

Figure 64. Cover of "Catalogue" for the second Arts and Crafts Exhibition, 1889, designed by Walter Crane.

In his book *Ideals in Art*, Walter Crane, the Society's first president, wrote, "We desired first of all to give opportunity to the designer and craftsman to exhibit their work to the public for its artistic interest and thus to assert the claims of decorative art and handicraft to attention equally with the painter of easel pictures, hitherto almost exclusively associated with the term art in the public mind. Ignoring the artificial distinction between Fine and Decorative art, we felt that the real distinction was what we conceived to be between good and bad art, or false and true taste and methods in handicraft, considering it of little value to endeavor to classify art according to its commercial value or social importance, while everything depended upon the spirit as well as the skill and fidelity with which the conception was expressed, in whatever material, seeing that a worker earned the title of artist by the sympathy with and treatment of his material, by due recognition of its capacity, and its natural limitations, as well as of the relation of the work to use and life."

The first Exhibition, in 1888, was held at the New Gallery. The Selecting Committee of the Society chose the exhibitors. This committee was made up of W.A.S. Benson, the metalwork designer; Walter Crane; Lewis F. Day; Mervyn Macartney, who was a designer and architect; William Morris; Heywood Sumner, the illustrator; and Stephen Webb, a furniture designer. Advertisements were run in newspapers and journals inviting entries. A book accompanying the exhibition contained articles by prominent designers in their own fields, such as an article about bookbinding by Emery Walker and about wallpapers by Walter Crane. Lectures and demonstrations (William Morris weaving, for example) also were given during the exhibition.

Unlike at the Home Art and Industries Association's shows, or the Haslemere Peasant shows later, the work at the Arts and Crafts Exhibitions was considered professional quality. This raised the status of embroidery to an art.

Probably the most important embroidery exhibited in 1888 was a screen designed by Mackmurdo, which had been made in 1884 (see Figure 65). As with other works by Mackmurdo (a very famous chair, for example, or his title page for *Wren's City Churches*, called by the art critic Pevsner the first work of art nouveau), the design of the embroidered screen shows prototypical elements of art nouveau.

Figure 65. Embroidered screen by Mackmurdo displayed at the Arts & Crafts Exhibition 1888. *The Studio Volume 16.*

At the second Exhibition, there was a special room for the display of embroidery. William Morris had proposed such in 1889. That is probably why 111 women showed embroidery (out of 593 exhibitors total). The most commented on work was done by May Morris and Una Ashworth Taylor.

Una Ashworth Taylor was the daughter of a poet and author (Sir Henry Taylor) with aristocratic connections and Irish ancestry. The household hosted many artistic and literary luminaries, including Robert Louis Stevenson, Gladstone, Tennyson, Thomas Carlyle, and Julia Margaret Cameron. G.F. Watts painted Una's mother and Charles Dodgson photographed Una and her brother. Una grew up to be known for her art needlework but was mostly known for writing novels and other literary works. She never married and lived with her unmarried sister.

The embroidery by Una Taylor was an Irish Nationalist banner designed by Walter Crane and given to Charles Stewart Parnell, the Irish Home Rule leader and politician, which was also embroidered with his signature. Most of the notice taken of it in the press of the time referred to it as unattractive. *The Saturday Review of Politics, Literature, Science, and Art* wrote, "We hope that it is not political bias that makes us think this flag of the future one of the most grotesque and hideous objects we ever saw. There is but little of the emerald about it; but as the Catalogue describes it, 'Sunburst breaking into Celtic cross, enclosed by Irish harp,' is the central idea of the design." *The Academy* wrote that the design "scarcely shows the decorative genius of Mr. Walter Crane at his best." *The Nation* referred to "the extraordinarily ugly Irish national banner, designed by Walter Crane, executed by Una Taylor, and exhibited by Charles Stewart Parnell, with a Celtic cross of flames enclosing the national harp..." *The Artist* said that the banner was "particularly unpleasant in color."

You're dying to see it now, aren't you? Sadly, I have been unable to locate any pictures of this work and its current whereabouts, if any, are unknown. Instead, I can offer Figure 66, a beautifully drawn angel reposing under an orange tree. This work by Una Taylor, designed by W. Graham Robertson, was offered for sale at the 1903 Arts and Crafts Exhibition for £20.

The embroidery in the next few exhibitions was mostly more of the same. The 1890 exhibition lost money, so after that exhibitions were held every three years instead of every year.

Figure 66. Panel worked by Una Taylor, designed by W. Graham Robertson, offered for sale at the 1903 Arts and Crafts Exhibition. *Modern Decorative Art in England.*

Figure 67. *Joli de Coeur Rose*, embroidered panel worked by Una Taylor, designed by W. Graham Robertson, shown at the 1906 Arts and Crafts Exhibition. *The Studio Volume 37.*

Sir William Reynolds-Stephens (knighted 1931) is mostly today known as an important member of the New Sculpture movement, but he was also a painter and active in many branches of the decorative arts, including embroidery (often executed by his wife, Annie Reynolds-Stephens), metalwork, and furniture design. A. L. Baldry wrote in *The Studio* (volume 17, 1899), "It would, perhaps, be difficult to find a more instructive instance of the unrest of a nature dominated by the craving for a mastery over artistic methods than is provided by the career of Mr. W. Reynolds-Stephens. His experiences serve as a kind of object lesson in versatility ... All roads seem to him to be worth following if only they lead to a goal important enough to justify the expenditure of energy necessary for reaching it."

Figure 68. Decorative panel, circa 1900, is entirely stitched in silk threads and was designed by Robert A. Dawson. *Photo by Simone Chaves Kullberg.*

In 1906, Una Taylor showed another design by W. Graham Robertson (see Figure 67). This doesn't appear to have been a success. *House and Garden* wrote in May 1906, "... a pictorial panel entitled *Joli de Coeur Rose* ... is very beautiful work and the design has great charm, but is rather wanting in repose. The crimson clad figure stands out rather startlingly from a nearly white background." Lewis F. Day in *The Magazine of Fine Arts* dismissed it thus: "Miss Una Taylor's beautiful workmanship is thrown away upon a design more appropriate to a poster." The figure is good, but the lettering is awful.

I have not been able to find out much about the artist Robert A. Dawson, who designed embroidery while at the Royal College of Art around 1900. The sweet little angel in Figure 68 was designed by him.

Other designers whose work appeared in Arts and Crafts exhibitions included the sculptor W. Reynolds-Stephens. By the 1890s, exhibitions had made embroidery a respectable art again, so that men who were mostly known in other media had begun designing needlework. And of course, if the public knew a male designer had drawn the embroidery design, they'd be more likely to buy it and embroidery itself would be given more prestige as an art form.

The Studio (volume 18, 1900): "From his design the artist's wife has worked a tea-cozy in silks, part appliqué and part embroidery, on a bright green ground. Founded upon the dandelion, no better instance could be desired of the adaptation of natural forms to ornamental purposes. [See Figure 69.] Two additional embroideries by Mrs. Reynolds-Stephens, from Mr. Voysey's designs, are a circular cushion, with swallows perched on berry-bearing branches [see Figure 70], and another, mounted so as to form a banner-screen. It is a striking and characteristic pattern—viz., a secretary-bird, serrated leaf turned over repeatedly, and delicate conventional blossoms and tendrils. The whole is of silk, and is carried out mainly in appliqué, upon an indigo blue ground [see Figure 71]."

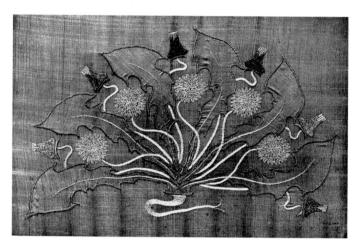

Figure 69. Silk dandelion tea cozy, designed by William Reynolds-Stephens, worked by Annie Reynolds-Stephens. *The Studio Volume 18.*

Figure 71. Silk embroidered and appliqué banner, designed by CFA Voysey, worked by Annie Reynolds-Stephens. *The Studio Volume 18.*

Figure 70. Embroidered cushion designed by CFA Voysey, worked by Annie Reynolds-Stephens. *The Studio Volume 18.*

So who *is* this Voysey fellow?

In 1903, *House & Garden* noted, "Mr. Voysey occupies a position in decorative art entirely to himself. He has had many followers, and is unquestionably a designer of singular originality and power." Preeminently an architect, C.F.A. Voysey was also a master of the decorative arts, designing furniture, carpets, wallpaper, metalware, and pretty much anything else, including a few very striking needlework designs, often executed by Mrs. Reynolds-Stephens. His style is deceptively simple, often including his distinctive birds, hearts, trees, and foliage. Unfortunately, extant examples of his designs in needlework are practically nonexistent today. Figure 72 shows a fire screen with an Adam & Eve design and Figure 73 an appliquéd work with a charming peasant couple.

Figure 72. Silk embroidery on linen ground designed by C.F.A. Voysey mounted as a fire screen. *Courtesy Netherhampton Salerooms.*

Figure 73. Appliqué and embroidered peasant couple on linen, designed by C.F.A. Voysey. *Modern Decorative Art in England.*

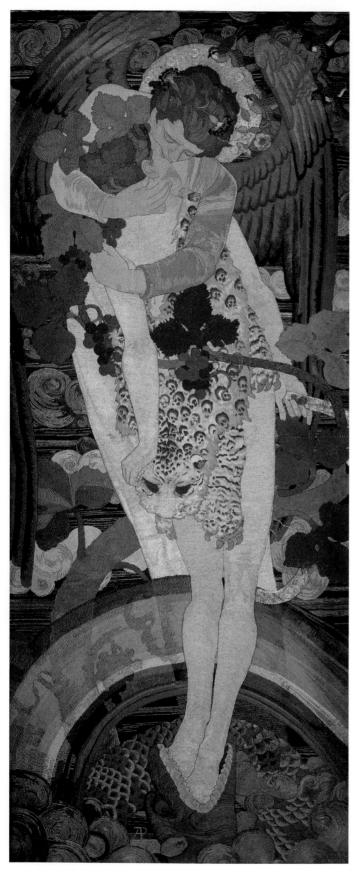

Figure 74. *The Victory*, silk and gold thread embroidered on linen, by Phoebe Anna Traquair, 1902. *Courtesy National Galleries of Scotland.*

Phoebe Traquair was, like Voysey, another of those giants of decorative arts, so it's difficult to sum up her work succinctly. Elizabeth Cumming, the art writer, calls her "the first important professional woman artist of modern Scotland." She was born in Dublin but moved to Edinburgh when she married paleontologist Dr. Ramsay Heatley Traquair. Part of the Scottish Arts and Crafts movement distinct from the Glasgow Style, her best work was possibly in enamels. In 1903, she exhibited a monumental set of embroidery panels, *The Progress of a Soul*, at the Arts and Crafts Exhibition. Figure 74 shows one of them, *The Victory*. This set of panels was for sale at £1000, but given that today they're in the National Galleries of Scotland, obtained by a bequest from the artist, I don't think they sold.

The set of panels took seven years to complete (they are six feet high and the four panels together are more than nine feet wide). The Christian soul is represented by a young man based on the character Denys L'Auxerrois from *Imaginary Portraits* by the English critic Walter Pater. (The character is a retelling of the Dionysus myth, with elements of Apollo, and is killed at the end. Oscar Wilde pointed out in the *Pall Mall Gazette* [1887] that the character itself was suggested to Walter Pater by needlework: "Denys l'Auxerrois is suggested by a figure found, or said to be found, on some old tapestries in Auxerre." How does Traquair get from the Dionysus myth to the Christian soul being brought aloft into heaven? Uh … that's art for you.) Not everyone was a fan. Lewis F. Day wrote that "Mrs. Traquair […] goes near enough to success in her endeavor to justify the place of honor allotted to her …" (*Art Journal*, March 1903.)

Grace Christie (Mrs. Archibald H. Christie) was an embroidery writer and teacher who exhibited her work at the Arts and Crafts Exhibitions. She was the only woman hired by William Lethaby as the head of the School of Design to teach at the Royal College of Art. In 1911, *Every Woman's Encyclopedia* (volume 5) published the following, "The Embroidery Class, which takes place on Thursday afternoons, under the direction of Mrs. Archibald H. Christie, is attended by almost every woman student in the school, for the demands for design and embroidery go together in almost every woman teacher's post, and girls double their chances of success if they are skilled in the intricacies of embroidery. There is a constant demand for teachers of embroidery and design from the trade schools, for which the salaries offered are from £130 to £150 a year. The Embroidery Class in full swing is specially interesting to the visitor, for each one of the forty or fifty students present is engaged in carrying out an original design, which she has herself executed after a thorough study of the masterpieces of old-world needlework in the museums, and many of the specimens which the writer was privileged to see were exquisite in design, coloring, and workmanship. The course includes the tracing of patterns, ancient and modem stitches and methods of work, gold work, figure work." Part of a sampler known as *The Wayside*, published in her book *Samplers and Stitches* (1920), is pictured in Figure 75.

Figure 75. Hedgehog from a sampler called *The Wayside*. *Samplers and Stitches*.

Mackay Hugh Baillie Scott was born in Kent, England, son of a wealthy Scottish landowner with interests in Australia. He attended an agricultural college to prepare to manage the family sheep stations in Australia, but then he became articled to an architect. He worked on the Isle of Man where he got to know a fellow art student, Archibald Knox,

the Liberty designer who influenced his work. His architecture is similar in many respects to Voysey's, while his decorative arts are similar to Voysey's and also Knox's. His work was sold through Liberty's as well as John P. White's furniture shop. The house he designed at Blackwell, Cumbria, is now a museum.

He had decided opinions on everything, including embroidery, as we've seen. Two examples of his work can be found in Figures 76 and 77. Notice the Voysey-esque plump little birds.

Figure 77. Embroidered and appliquéd panel designed by Baillie Scott. *The Studio Volume 28.*

Figure 76. Embroidered and appliquéd screen panels designed by Baillie Scott. *The Studio Volume 28.*

Haslemere Peasant Industries

Haslemere Peasant Industries in Surrey was a marketing organization for Surrey craftspeople started by Godfrey Blount in 1894 (see Figure 78). It was run by three related families who believed that traditional craft skills were dying out in the countryside and who wanted to restore "country life, its faith and its craft." A London shop sold these craft goods, as did one in Haslemere.

Figure 78. Making hand-tufted carpets and peasant tapestry at Haslemere, *The Art Journal Volume 68.*

Stewart Dick wrote in *The Craftsman* in 1907 that "A social reformer as well as an artist and craftsman, Mr. Blount is a sincere disciple of Ruskin, and an eloquent preacher of the gospel of simplicity alike in life and in handicraft. […]

"The Peasants' Arts Society is carried on by Mr. Blount and his wife, as directors, and most of the actual work is done by young girls of the neighborhood. Mr. Blount is also the designer and controls the artistic side of the industry. It is not a cooperative institution, the capital being supplied by Mr. Blount, and the labor being paid, at so much per hour, but the workers, clean, fresh, country girls, are happy in the work and devoted to their employers. The society is purely philanthropic in this respect— that no private profits are taken from it, all such profits going to further the work and increase its scope. On the other hand, care is taken to price work at its proper commercial value, so as to maintain a right standard and in no way to undersell individual craftsmen."

Godfrey Blount (1859-1931) was an artist who trained at the Slade School and who designed most of the "tapestries" for Haslemere. His wife often did the embroidery. Ethel Blount wrote, "We have all been robbed of most of the things which make life happy. Materialism has stolen our ancient joys and privileges, our traditions of dress, food, craft, and amusements (not to speak of yet nobler things), and it is women, mainly, who will have to fight for them and recapture them for the world, if we are ever to have them again. But they must do it in earnest and wholeheartedly. They must reconquer the ancient crafts of the home, remaking the home the center of creativeness and pleasure; they must forgo the worship of fashion, and no longer clothing themselves, as kaleidoscopes, with eternal change of meaningless colors and shapes, they must wear the beautiful stuffs that their hands have made, and clothe their household in them: they must make the bread their children eat, and in a thousand ways affirm the truths that imaginative hand-labor is honorable, and that all true life can, and should, be sacramental."

Figure 79. Screen designed by Godfrey Blount for appliqué and embroidery. *The Studio Volume 9.*

Most of the "peasant embroideries" were appliquéd linen on linen with linen thread. They were used as wall hangings, *portières* (door curtains), casement curtains, and bed hangings. They were very fashionable in artistic circles. The screen in Figure 79 was shown at the Home Arts and Industries Association at the Royal Albert Hall, 1897, while Figure 80 is a work by Godfrey Blount that was shown at the Arts and Crafts Exhibition in 1906 called *The Spies*.

M.H. Baillie Scott wrote in *The Studio*, Volume 28 (1903), "The most direct method of appliqué is to sew on the pieces with invisible thread, merely turning in the edges of the material. The next process is that which is sometimes called 'peasant embroidery,' probably because it is seldom practiced by peasants and cannot be strictly described as embroidery. [Snuh-ap, Baillie Scott!] In this the outline is made a feature in the design, and, like the lead line in a stained glass window, separates the different materials."

Stewart Dick also noted that a feature of the peasant embroidery was its simplicity. "The forms are kept large and simple, the finished articles being intended for wall coverings, curtains, coverlets, table cloths and such like, where a broad effect is more desirable than fine detail."

The peasant embroideries were exhibited often at Home Arts Industries shows and were used by Wylie & Lochhead at their stand at the 1901 Glasgow Exhibition (see Figure 81). (The bed covering is Haslemere. I actually think it clashes rather badly with the delicate furniture.)

Blount was also a deeply religious man. He founded the Fellowship of the New Crusade, which encouraged simple living and traditional country crafts and pastimes. He also started a country church where he preached on Sundays. In 1927 Blount founded the Supernatural Society to counter materialism with simple living and Christian beliefs. He died in 1937.

Figure 80. Peasant tapestry designed by Godfrey Blount, worked by Mrs. Joseph King. *The Art Journal Volume 68.*

Figure 81. Bedroom, designed by George Logan, Glasgow International Exhibition, 1901. *Hulton Archive/Getty Images.*

Bromsgrove Guild

The Bromsgrove Guild of Applied Arts was founded in 1898. It grew out of the Bromsgrove School of Art. The school wanted to create a commercial enterprise where its graduates could sell their work (see Figure 82).

Its headmaster, Walter Gilbert, described the Guild in *The Craftsman* (1903): "The members of the Guild are individuals who have advanced beyond the limits of 'professionalism', that they might adopt the more prolific method of thinking and working in their media. These men and women, while they stand pledged to cooperation and mutual support, have individual studios and workshops altogether independent. Each department is financed and controlled separately by the guildsmen of the same department who train their apprentices: choosing and employing only those who are capable of developing the main idea of the master craftsman."

In the early years, members worked from their own studios around England, while Gilbert managed its output from Bromsgrove.

The Guild is best known today for its metalwork, particularly wrought iron. It made the main gates of Buckingham Palace and the Liver Birds of The Royal Liver Assurance Building in Liverpool. But guild members also were known for plasterwork, wood carving, stained glass, and mural decoration. And unlike many other companies associated with the Arts and Crafts Movement, the Bromsgrove Guild had a long history, finally winding up in 1966.

In embroidery, the Guild's best known member was Mary J. Newill (1860-1947). Mary Newill worked as a painter, illustrator, embroiderer, and stained glass designer. She studied at Birmingham School of Art and subsequently taught embroidery there from 1892 until 1919. In addition to the Bromsgrove Guild, she was a member of the Arts and Crafts Exhibition Society and showed her embroidery at its fifth exhibition in 1896.

The embroidered panels in Figures 83 and 84 were featured in the Bromsgrove Guild's display at the *Exposition Universelle et Internationale* in Paris in 1900, where Newill was awarded a bronze medal.

Figure 82. Advertisement for the Bromsgrove Guild. *The Studio Volume 18.*

Figure 83. Embroidered and appliquéd panel, worked in colored silks on unbleached linen, by Mary J. Newill, c. 1899, entitled "The House of Holiness." *Courtesy of Lyon & Turnbull.*

Figure 84. Embroidered and appliquéd panel, worked in colored silks on unbleached linen, by Mary J. Newill, c. 1899, entitled "The Wandering Wood." *Courtesy of Lyon & Turnbull.*

These panels, based on Spenser's *Faerie Queen*, were originally designed for a dining room. *The Studio* wrote of this work that Newill wanted to "emulate the effect of Japanese prints" using broad panels of appliqué. To me, they look like a book illustration possibly by Burne-Jones or Walter Crane (who admired Newill's work). Another panel designed for the same room is shown in Figure 85. You can see the panels in situ in Figures 86 and 87. They were made for Mr. Edmund Butler's house, Top O' the Hill, in Sutton Coldfield.

Figure 86. Mary J. Newill's embroidered panels in situ, dining room, c. 1901. *Modern British Domestic Architecture and Decoration.*

Figure 85. Embroidered and appliquéd panel, worked in colored silks, by Mary J. Newill, c. 1899, entitled "The Garden of Adonis." *Modern British Domestic Architecture and Decoration.*

Figure 87. Mary J. Newill's embroidered panels in situ, dining room, c. 1901. *Modern British Domestic Architecture and Decoration.*

Figure 88. Panel by Mary J. Newill, *Gareth and Lionors. The Studio Volume 28.*

The Craftsman commented in May 1903, "In the department of embroidery the Bromsgrove Guild has produced several notable works. Among such is a series of panels designed for the decoration of a dining room. The ground of the panels is in light chocolate color, with the design worked out in green serge appliqué for foliage, and in light linen for the figures and buildings, while the outlines and certain details are done in embroidery. By this means, which is a combination of two methods: appliqué and the more elaborate needlework, excellent results are obtained without great effort, and it becomes possible to undertake extensive schemes of decoration at a very moderate cost."

The Burne-Jones influence is even more evident in Figure 88, a panel depicting Gareth and Lionors (from *Le Morte d'Arthur*), which was shown at the seventh Arts and Crafts Exhibition in 1903. The Studio referred to it as "archaic and arras-like" and "ambitious and scholarly."

Figure 89 shows a banner executed by Newill for the Sherbourne Road Girls' School that was pictured in the 1909 *Studio Yearbook of Decorative Arts*. Compare and contrast with the Liberty & Co. embroidery in Figure 133 (p. 69). I'd guess Mary Newill also sold needlework designs to Liberty's. The Liberty embroidery book must have been published in 1917 or later; before then, Liberty's postal code would have been W, not W1.

Figure 89. Embroidered and appliquéd panel by Mary J. Newill. *Studio Year-book of Decorative Arts, 1909.*

The Clarion Guild of Handicrafts

The Clarion was a weekly socialist newspaper started by Robert Blatchford in 1891. It published work by George Bernard Shaw and Walter Crane. Eventually, though, Blatchford annoyed readers with support for the Boer War and opposition to women's suffrage. After World War I, the paper moved further to the right, finally ceasing publication in 1931.

The Clarion women's page was written by Julia Dawson, who in 1901 suggested that the paper start a handicrafts guild. Stewart Dick wrote in *The Craftsman* in 1905: "It is essentially a working-man's guild. There are no high fees; there are no paid teachers. The more expert members, and the Guild includes many first rate craftsmen, place their services at the disposal of the less skillful, and the weekly subscriptions only amount to a few pence per member, to meet the cost of such necessary items as rent, light and heating. This no doubt sounds Utopian, but it works well in practice; a fine feeling of *esprit de corps* animates the different branches; and in addition to turning out good work, each branch forms a pleasant and stimulating social center."

Embroidery was popular in the Clarion Guild. Dick says, "A section particularly attractive to ladies was that devoted to embroideries. In this field there seems to be a growing tendency to turn from the old minute work to the bolder and more striking effects which are obtained in appliqué, and which lend themselves so well to the decoration of portières or other large hangings. It is particularly pleasing to see the revival of this ancient art, which seems so particularly a woman's art, and in which such delightful effects can be obtained."

In the exhibition of 1905, Ann Macbeth, Phoebe McLeish, and Lily Yeats showed their work (see Figures 90 and 91). Ann Macbeth also sent her designs to be used by workers.

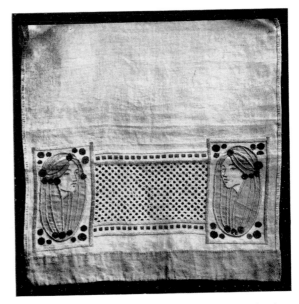

Figure 90. Embroidered sachet by Ann Macbeth. *The Studio Volume 28.*

Figure 91. *The Meadow*, designed by E.C. Yeats and embroidered by Lily Yeats. *The Art Journal Volume 68.*

Not everyone was a fan, however. The rival socialist newspaper *The New Age* huffed in 1907: "If the exhibition is intended as a foretaste of what art will be like under Socialism, I can only say that I do not like it. Apart from the work of a dozen or so exhibitors—professional craftsmen who have no particular concern with the Clarion Guild—the work exhibited is mostly rubbish. I should have been glad to dissemble my disapproval in vague phrases, but the painful fact is that nothing short of the naked truth will suffice to convey my meaning to people who have so completely misunderstood the intentions of Morris and the pioneers of our handicraft revival." But the *British Journal of Nursing* stated, "The Clarion Guild of Handicraft [...] consists of associations of men and women, many of whom are employed during the day in uncongenial tasks, and who in their scanty leisure meet together at a common workroom to find solace in the work they love for its own sake. The beautiful work [...] here shown, goes far to prove that the finest work is done by those who can give effect to their desire to produce the best that is in them."

Women's Guild of Arts

May Morris founded the Women's Guild of Arts in 1907. There were no decorative arts organizations at the time that admitted women, nor would most for many years to come. Mary Newill was another member. Unfortunately, there isn't much information available about this group, but we do know that it gave lectures and offered events to appeal to craftswomen. The Guild contributed a bedroom to the Arts and Crafts Exhibition of 1916, with embroidered cushions, bed covers, and hangings. Furniture was by Ernest Gimson and some embroidery done by the Birmingham Guild. The exhibition catalog referred to it as a "Lady's bedroom in which elaboration and luxury have been purposely avoided." *The Studio* noted sarcastically that not all the exhibits were priced, but for those that were, the total approached £500; the bed and hangings alone were £170.

Other Work

As we've seen, medieval designs were very popular among English Arts and Crafts designers. Not so much in Scotland, as much of medieval Scotland was filled with clan wars rather than rural idyll. Figure 92 shows a charming embroidered medieval farming scene. The figures do look like they were drawn by a Scottish designer, and the castle looks vaguely like Glamis in Scotland, but I'm going to assume it's an English work anyway.

Figure 92. Medieval scene, silk embroidery on linen. Notice the finely embroidered ears of wheat.

Figure 93 is an embroidered panel for a piano front, designed by Herbert Sershall, worked by Mrs. H. Sershall (do you think the H stands for Herbert?), featuring medieval ladies.

Galleons were a popular motif, as shown in illuminated manuscripts. They symbolized the passing of time, the fleeting nature of life. The banner in Figure 94 was designed by a Miss W. Freeman, and shown at an exhibition of Arts and Crafts at the Lyceum Club in 1906.

Figure 94. Embroidered panel by Miss W. Freeman. *The Studio Volume 36.*

More pretty medieval ladies are shown in Figures 95 and 96. Figure 95 was entered in a competition by the Royal School of Art Needlework, circa 1890. Figure 96 is a silk triptych depicting Saint Frideswyde, Saint Elizabeth, and Saint Bridget.

Figure 93. Embroidered panel for a piano front, designed by Herbert Sershall, worked by Mrs. H. Sershall. *Modern Decorative Art in England.*

Figure 95. Embroidered wall hanging entered in a competition by the Royal School of Art Needlework, circa 1890. *Photo by Simone Chaves Kullberg.*

Figure 96. Embroidered silk triptych by Ethell Darton, circa 1905. *Courtesy Hill House Antiques.*

More pretty ladies are up next. Figures 97 through 100 are painted and embroidered panels personifying the seasons, while Figure 101 is a silkwork illustration of the line "My heart is like a singing bird," from the poem "A Birthday" by Christina Rossetti.

Figure 98. *Spring*, embroidered and painted silk picture, c. 1904. *Courtesy Jan Edwards.*

Figure 99. *Summer*, embroidered and painted silk picture, c. 1904. *Courtesy Jan Edwards.*

Figure 97. *Winter*, embroidered and painted silk picture, c. 1904. *Courtesy Jan Edwards.*

Figure 100. *Autumn*, embroidered and painted silk picture, c. 1904. *Courtesy Jan Edwards.*

Figure 102. Silk embroidered panel, *The Rose Bower*, by Miss Joan Drew, c. 1905. *The Studio Volume 38.*

Figure 102 is a panel entitled *The Rose Bower* by Miss Joan Drew, c. 1905. *The Studio* mentioned "the singularly successful attempt the artist has made to bring within the limitations of her difficult medium all possible effect of variety and vibration of color, and thus to attain a decorative charm such as will appeal to the eye of an artist, but which we remark is seldom captured within the precise and decorative laws which govern the art of needlework."

Tired of pretty ladies? How about some flowers? First up are some designs from DMC. Wait, isn't DMC French? Yes, but their designs were and are known worldwide. DMC (Dollfus Mieg & Cie) was founded in 1746 to print fabrics in what was then the Alsace region of Switzerland (and was annexed by France in 1798). In 1841, the company began producing thread. The company bought the patent rights to a process called mercerization. Mercerized cotton is dipped into a caustic alkali solution, which makes it stronger, shinier, and easier to dye. This meant that mercerized cotton could compete with silk in appearance, while being much cheaper.

DMC became a huge international supplier of thread (as it remains today). DMC published an *Encyclopedia of Needlework* by Austria's Theresa von Dillmont, which remained a best-seller for one hundred years, and also produced catalogs of needlework designs, something we'll see repeated by American thread companies (see Figure 103).

Figure 101. *My Heart Is Like a Singing Bird*, silk embroidery on silk satin, c. 1905. *Courtesy Jan Edwards.*

Figure 103. Catalogs from various embroidery thread companies.

Early catalogs by DMC show a lot of Arts and Crafts and art nouveau influence. Figures 104 through 106 show particularly attractive floral designs by DMC.

Figure 104. Design for embroidery from *Motifs for Embroideries*, IInd Series, DMC.

Figure 105. Design for embroidery from *Motifs for Embroideries*, IInd Series, DMC.

Figure 106. Design for embroidery from *Motifs for Embroideries*, IInd Series, DMC.

An English art needlework catalog produced by the English Sewing Cotton Company Ltd., Manchester, c. 1900, furnished the design in Figure 107, a chair back called *Pansy and Butterfly*. As you'll see below, thread companies in America began to merge after World War I. In Britain, the giant thread companies Coats and Clarks merged in 1896; in response, fourteen firms merged to create the rival English Sewing Cotton Company, Ltd. in 1897.

Figure 107. *Pansy and Butterfly* design from *Art Needlework* catalog, published by English Sewing Cotton Company.

Figure 108 is a piece of linen provided with my September 1902 issue of *The House: The Journal of Home Arts & Crafts: a Monthly for the Artistic Home.* Nice design, but no one could be bothered to embroider it in the past 110 years. Figure 109 is a stylized flower design on a drawstring bag. A later, more Jacobean style of embroidery is shown in Figure 110, which was designed by G. Ll. Morris and sewn by Winifred Morris.

Figure 108. Linen embroidery design from *The House: The Journal of Home Arts & Crafts.*

Figure 109. Linen drawstring bag with cotton perle thread.

Figure 110. Embroidered hanging designed by G. Ll. Morris and sewn by Winifred Morris. *Modern Decorative Art in England.*

The attractive crib blanket in Figure 111 was designed and made by Frances Jones, a student at the Liverpool School of Art, and was exhibited around 1903. *The Studio* said that, "The design and execution of embroidery has become a leading feature in this school ... Several excellent cot covers, some in silk upon linen, and some in embroidered appliqué, are worked by Frances Jones ..."

I love the stylized blackberry (or bramble) tree in Figure 112. Figure 113 is also stylized, with flowers in a sort of Glasgow design in peaches and teals.

Birds were also popular designs. Figure 114 shows an appliquéd hanging by Goodyers of Regent Street, a London department store. The furniture and designs that appear in the *Studio Year-book* of 1906 by Goodyers are assumed to be by the Glasgow architect George Walton, a contemporary and rival of Charles Rennie Mackintosh's, so I attribute these hangings to him. Pictures of furniture by Walton appear in Goodyers' design books.

Figure 112. Embroidered blackberry design panel. *Courtesy Jan Edwards.*

Figure 111. Embroidered crib blanket by Frances Jones. *The Studio Volume 31.*

Figure 113. Floral design panel, silk on linen. *Courtesy Jan Edwards.*

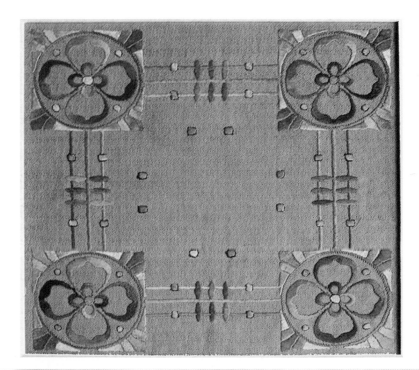

Figure 114. Appliqué hanging by Goodyers of Regent Street. *1906 Studio Year-Book of Decorative Arts*

The rather attractive fire screen in Figure 115 is dated circa 1905. I love the bird in the tree and the fish in the stream.

Figure 115. Silk and appliqué embroidered fire screen, c. 1905. *Courtesy Jan Edwards.*

Chapter 5

Liberty & Co.

Arthur Lasenby Liberty opened his shop on Regent Street on May 17, 1875. While manager at Farmer's and Roger's Oriental Warehouse, a meeting place for artists, Liberty told customers like Whistler that when he had his own shop, he would change the fashion in dress and decoration.

The name Liberty became a byword for good taste in upper middle-class Victorian life (see Figure 116, a cartoon from *Punch*, 1894). At first Mr. Liberty only sold goods that he imported or bought-in; but from the 1880s, Liberty commissioned fabrics designed by leading artists such as Walter Crane and Christopher Dresser; furniture, metalware, jewelry, glassware, and so on soon followed. The "Liberty Art Fabrics" were soon the height of Aesthetic Movement fashion. Liberty textiles were and are prized for their softness and good draping qualities.

The fashion and embroidery departments have always been among the most important at Liberty's. Liberty's costume department was established in 1884, with architect E.W. Godwin as first director. He'd designed artistic dresses for his lover, Ellen Terry, the Victorian era's most famous actress.

The Liberty workrooms created dresses that defied Paris fashion; many of Liberty's artistic dresses continued to be offered virtually unchanged, in some cases for at least twenty years.

In an 1896 catalog, Liberty dresses are stated to be "selected and designed from the most beautiful examples in the past history of costume. They combine refinement with distinction and are always in fashion." John Ruskin, the art critic, wrote that historical dress has had more time to be "perfected" and was therefore superior to the frivolous fashions of the day.

FELICITOUS QUOTATIONS.

Hostess (of Upper Tooting, showing new house to Friend). "WE'RE VERY PROUD OF THIS ROOM, MRS. HOMINY. OUR OWN LITTLE UPHOLSTERER DID IT UP JUST AS YOU SEE IT, AND ALL OUR FRIENDS THINK IT WAS *LIBERTY!*"
Visitor (sotto voce). "'OH, LIBERTY, LIBERTY, HOW MANY CRIMES ARE COMMITTED IN THY NAME!'"

Figure 116. Cartoon from *Punch* by George du Maurier, October 20, 1894.

The coat in Figures 117 and 118 is in the Empire style popularized by Josephine of France one hundred years before. Yet the embroidery recalls medieval Europe. This is the *Marion Visiting Coat* as shown in Liberty's 1905 *Dress and Decoration* catalog and in an extant garment. The coat is made of satin with lambswool padding, with a medieval-style embroidered border in black silk floss and seed beads. The buttons are also embroidered. The *"Amelia Empire Evening Gown with Coat … embroidered in harmonious coloring"* is shown in Figure 119. I painted my living room blue and green based entirely on my desire to be the lady in that picture. So far all I've got is her Tudric pewter vase, though.

Sometimes Liberty stopped hinting at medieval and just went for it entirely. *Iseult* is the name of the dress in Figure 120, a "French 14th Century Evening Gown," with appliqué and hand embroidery.

Figure 118. *Marion Visiting Coat* pictured in Liberty's 1905 *Dress and Decoration* catalog.

Figure 117. Liberty & Co. *Marion Visiting Coat*, of black Orion satin softly constructed with lambswool padding through torso and long sleeves, the sleeves shirred at cap and cuff, wide square pilgrim style collar, cuffs, and soft high-waisted belt of ecru satin with concentric rows of embroidered black silk floss and clear glass seed beads, each with a medieval motif border in the same. *Courtesy Doyle New York.*

Figure 119. *Amelia Empire Evening Gown with Coat* from Liberty's 1905 *Dress and Decoration* catalog.

Figure 120. *Iseult* evening gown from Liberty's 1905 *Dress and Decoration* catalog.

According to Anna Buruma, current Liberty & Co. archivist, "Although there is no mention in the catalogues of the dresses being embroidered to order there are various examples where the same embroidery patterns are used on different dresses and it is possible that embroidery samples or artwork were available for customers to choose from." (*Decorative Arts Society Journal*, 2009.) She also points out that by 1902, twenty-nine people worked in the costume department, while thirty-one worked in the furniture department, not counting workroom hands or factory workers. Clearly, the dress department was a very important part of Liberty's business.

"Oriental" (non-Western) styles of clothing were favored by artistic dressers. Velvet opera coats or capes known as "burnouses," lavishly embroidered, were particularly fashionable and popular. The burnous (a.k.a. burnoose) is an Arabic hooded cloak, often decorated with embroidery and tassels. The garment became fashionable in the 1850s; the loose folds were easy to wear over crinolines and the hoods could be worn over bonnets or instead of bonnets. *Everybody's Magazine* (1905) wrote, "Ever since the French entered Algiers [1830], the Arabian burnous has furnished a motif for the French coat makers."

The burnous was less popular in the 1880s and 1890s, when more fitted garments were in style, except among Aesthetic fashions, which demanded looser silhouettes and emphasized exotic, "Oriental" silhouettes. The burnous became more popular in the early twentieth century. Some examples from Liberty & Co. survive, of which Figure 121 is one of the prettiest.

This example is made of wisteria silk velvet with old-rose silk satin lining. The cocoon shape and hip buttons make me date it around 1913, when Paul Poiret set the fashion for that silhouette. Note the classic Arts and Crafts pomegranates in the embroidery.

Figure 122 is a burnous-styled cape, c. 1905, in pink cashmere. The embroidery trimming recalls both Liberty's art nouveau metalware and the inlay on some of its Arts and Crafts furniture. The velvet opera coat in Figure 123 is embellished with Arts and Crafts Tudor rose embroidery.

Figure 122. Evening cloak by Liberty & Co., cashmere with velvet appliqué and silk embroidery. © *Cheltenham Art Gallery & Museums, Gloucestershire, UK / The Bridgeman Art Library.*

Figure 121. Liberty & Co. velvet burnous circa 1910, silk velvet with silk satin lining, shawl collar with elongated ecclesiastical point at rear concluding in a knotted silk tassel, embroidered with wisteria silk floss and bronzed metallic thread in a foliate design incorporating pomegranates. *Courtesy Doyle New York.*

Figure 123. Velvet Liberty & Co. coat circa 1900, featuring Tudor rose embroidery and metallic beads. *Photo by Simone Chaves Kullberg.*

Figure 124. Close up of embroidered and smocked Liberty & Co. silk dress, c. 1909. *Courtesy Kerry Taylor Auctions.*

Liberty clothing often featured embroidery in the same color as the garment. Figure 124 is a close up of the gown in Figure 125, a smocked garment that seems to have been popular for at least twenty years. I am dating this dress c. 1909 based on the sleeves and the yoke; a similar smocked design with leg o'mutton sleeves appeared in an 1893 catalog called *Evolution in Costume illustrated by Past Fashion Plates and Present Adaptions of the Empire and the Early Victorian Period.* Figure 126 shows yet another version with bishop sleeves from the 1905 *Dress and Decoration* catalog. This is the "*Cecelia* English 17th Century Evening Gown Robe of soft silk smocked at the waist and neck."

Figure 125. Embroidered and smocked Liberty & Co. silk dress, c. 1909. *Courtesy Kerry Taylor Auctions.*

Figure 126. *Cecelia English 17th Century Evening Gown Robe* from Liberty's 1905 *Dress and Decoration* catalog.

Smocking became popular in the 1870s for women's and children's wear. The smock was a garment worn by working men in rural England from about 1750 to about 1850 (see Figure 127). It was a loose garment worn as a shirt or tunic, with gathers at the neckline and cuffs, often decorated with embroidery. The sewn gathers are known as smocking. These make the garment stretch with a woven fabric and yet make the neckline and cuffs less full—all important for a farm laborer or similar worker. The smocked gowns worn by artistic girls and children therefore recalled rural innocence and simplicity. (And just as smocking became popular for artistic dress, it died out for rural workers, who wanted more sophisticated clothing. William Morris sometimes worked in a smock, but even then it was thought to be slightly affected. Interestingly, smocks were still associated with rural simplicity in popular consciousness as late as 1970, when Monty Python portrayed hayseed yokels in smocks.)

Figure 127. Smock frock as worn by agricultural workers. *Embroidery: Or, the Craft of the Needle.*

Children's Dress

Smocking was thought especially appropriate for children's clothing because of its association with innocence. In fact, traditional little girls' dresses today are still often smocked. Liberty's stocked "Artistic Dress for Children" as early as 1884. The fashion for little girls' artistic clothing was set by the children's book illustrations of Kate Greenaway, who may have actually designed clothing for Liberty. Certainly, some of Liberty's styles were direct copies of those in Greenaway's illustrations. Many of Liberty's styles for girls featured the Empire styles that Greenaway made popular.

Embroidery was, of course, featured on Liberty children's clothing. In its *Fancy Dress for Children* catalog (1899), the *Freda* coat for girls ages four to seven is "in cloth, lined Liberty-silk, and collar hand-embroidered with silk."

Figures 128, 129, and 130 show two Liberty children's coats with embroidery, c. 1900. Even though Figure 129 is being modeled by a little girl, it may well have been designed for a boy. The flowers on Figure 130 particularly recall Jessie M. King's designs for Liberty Cymric silver and jewelry (see Figure 131); it's possible King designed this coat. She did design fabrics for Liberty.

Figure 129. Close up of Liberty & Co. embroidered wool coat.

Figure 130. Liberty & Co. wool coat lined with cotton, with embroidered yoke, cuffs, and buttons, c. 1900.

Figure 128. Liberty & Co. wool coat lined with cotton, with embroidered yoke, cuffs, and buttons, c. 1900. Three-year-old Aurora not included.

Figure 131. Silver and enamel buckle by Liberty & Co., designed by Jessie M. King. *Courtesy Tadema Gallery.*

Figure 132. *Marjorie* embroidered child's coat from Liberty's 1905 *Dress and Decoration* catalog.

Figure 132 shows the *Marjorie* from the *Dress and Decoration* catalog. Cuffs and cape are of embroidered silk; the design recalls the Tudor rose embroidery in Figure 123.

Embroidery

Liberty sold embroidery supplies almost from the very beginning. Figure 133 shows a design that looks very much like one by Mary J. Newill in Figure 89; in common with many firms of the time, Liberty did not identify its designers, preferring to have an anonymous house style, so it's not possible to know for sure in many cases who designed what.

Figure 133. Cover of Liberty embroidery designs catalog c. 1917.

Liberty's needlework school was set up in 1884 (it still exists today). Also like other firms of the time, Liberty sold transfer patterns for embroidery. It is known that Ann Macbeth designed for Liberty, and many of the patterns have a distinct Glasgow look to them (see Figure 134 and 135). Other designs that seem to have been very popular include nursery rhyme characters. Figures 136 and 137 shows the *Bo-Peep* design and one example of it; Figures 138 and 139 show the *Mary Quite Contrary* pattern and one executed version.

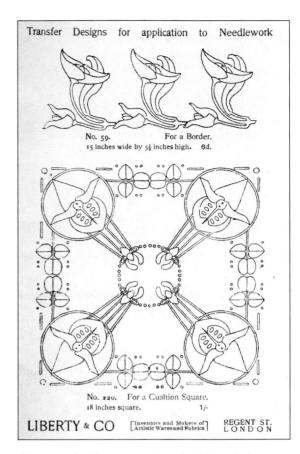

Figure 134. Glasgow style embroidery design from Liberty *Designs for Embroidery* catalog, c. 1900.

Figure 135. Glasgow style embroidery design from Liberty *Designs for Embroidery* catalog, c. 1900.

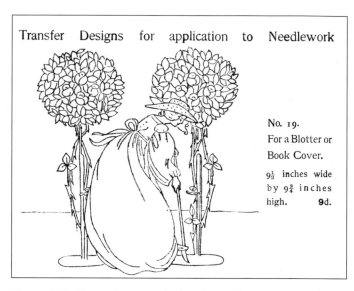

Figure 136. *Bo-Peep* design from Liberty *Designs for Embroidery* catalog, c. 1900.

Figure 138. *Quite Contrary* design from Liberty *Designs for Embroidery* catalog, c. 1900.

Figure 137. *Bo-Peep* embroidery in silk and appliqué. *Courtesy Jan Edwards.*

Figure 139. *Quite Contrary* embroidery in silk and appliqué. *Courtesy Jan Edwards.*

Liberty also sold embroidered items that were fully worked, including trinket boxes, picture frames, cushions, pincushions, work bags, blotters, and so on from about 1912 on, in a catalog called *Choice and Charming Presents*.

For more ambitious ladies, Liberty sold lengths of printed cotton to be worked at home. Figures 140, 141, and 142 show a rather lovely 1890s floral embroidered panel featuring tulips, peonies, daffodils, and roses in polychrome silk on a cream ground. These were produced by Thomas Wardle of Leek.

Figure 141. Close up of Leek embroidery design kit sold by Liberty & Co., c. 1890. *Courtesy Meg Andrews.*

Figure 140. Leek embroidery design kit sold by Liberty & Co., c. 1890. *Courtesy Meg Andrews.*

Figure 142. Close up of Leek embroidery design kit sold by Liberty & Co., c. 1890. *Courtesy Meg Andrews.*

Chapter 6

Glasgow Style

The Studio in 1910 summed up the Glasgow Style approach to design: "It is not founded on tradition and has no resemblance to any style that preceded it. The new embroidery is common in this respect to the oldest arts; it takes the everyday things in life, and by a simple individualistic process makes them beautiful as well as useful." Figures 143 to 145 shows three Glasgow Style designs by unknown makers.

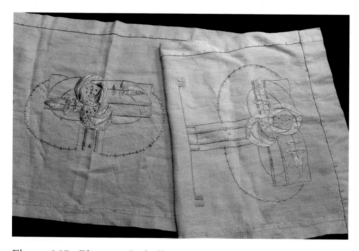

Figure 143. Glasgow Style linen runner, cotton thread.

Figure 144. Stenciled and embroidered Glasgow Style embroidery panel, rose tree design.

Figure 145. Mauve linen and silk appliqué Glasgow Style banner with silk embroidery. *Photo by Simone Chaves Kullberg.*

The embroidery department at the Glasgow School of Art developed an entirely new approach to the art. The head of the department was a remarkable woman called Jessie Newbery (see Figure 345).

Jessie Newbery is remembered today mainly for her exquisite embroidery, but she also worked in stained glass, metals, and enamels. Her father believed that women should be educated, so she went to boarding school and then to the Glasgow School of Art to, as she put it later, "perfect [her] drawing." But what she actually got at the school was a serious art education. She married the Headmaster of the School, Francis H. Newbery, in 1889.

In 1894, Mrs. Newbery established the department of embroidery at the Glasgow School of Art. Her innovative designs, based on her love of flowers and plants, eventually brought the embroidery department worldwide fame (see Figure 146). Mrs. Newbery expected her students, as artists, to design and execute their own work. Jessie Newbery taught design in the embroidery department, relying on others to teach technique. Under her guidance, the embroidery department became one of the most important at the school.

Figure 146. Embroidered silk picture by Jessie Newbery with openwork edging.

Figure 147. Embroidered banner by Ann Macbeth or Jessie Newbery. *The Studio Volume 24.*

Her ablest student, Ann Macbeth, succeeded her when she retired from the school after an illness in 1908. But she continued to embroider, exhibiting with the Scottish Guild of Handicraft and at the Louvre in 1914.

The other central figure in Glasgow Style embroidery, Ann Macbeth (see Figure 351), started teaching in the embroidery department while still a student. As a student, she became assistant to Jessie Newbery in 1901, helping out in the Needlework, Embroidery, and Appliqué class. In 1901, she designed a banner carrying Glasgow's coat of arms for the Exhibition of 1901 (see Figure 147). In 1902, again as a student, she won a silver medal at the Turin Exposition with her "Sleeping Beauty" embroidery. She also designed and made a silk cushion that was presented to Queen Alexandra for her coronation that featured the rose, leek, thistle, and shamrock of Britain.

After Mrs. Newbery gave up teaching in 1908, Miss Macbeth became the head of the embroidery department (the only woman to be called Professor at the school). She was one of the key figures in making the School of Art internationally renowned; she received honorary diplomas all over the world.

Figure 148 shows a figural panel, *The Annunciation*, almost certainly by Ann Macbeth. Figure 149 is another panel, *Caritas*, known to be by Ann Macbeth since it was pictured in *The Studio Volume 50.* Figure 150 is a tea cozy pattern attributed to Ann Macbeth. Figure 151 is a very large panel by Miss Macbeth, *The Queen of May*, depicted in the Studio Year-Book for 1914.

Figure 149. *Caritas*, a figural panel designed and executed by Ann Macbeth. Silk thread on silk satin backing with beads.

Figure 148. Silk and satin Glasgow Style embroidered picture. © *Christie's Images Ltd.*

Figure 150. Glasgow Style tea cozy design. *Art Needlework* catalog, published by English Sewing Cotton Company.

Figure 151. *The Queen of May*, large embroidered and appliquéd silk panel by Ann Macbeth.

It was as a teacher that Miss Macbeth made perhaps her most lasting contribution. Like Mrs. Newbery, she hated embroidery transfers and encouraged embroiderers to develop their own designs. She developed new techniques for teaching needlecraft to children. She also wrote numerous books, including *Educational Needlecraft, The Playwork Book, Embroidered Lace and Leatherwork, Needleweaving,* and *The Countrywoman's Rug Book.*

Eventually Miss Macbeth retired to Patterdale in Cumbria, visiting Glasgow to teach sometimes. The local church, St. Patrick's, contains some of her designs (see Figure 152). She was well-known personally for her kindness and her encouraging "Try it, ladies, of course you can do it."

Figure 152. Banner embroidered by Ann Macbeth. *Courtesy of St. Patrick's Church, Patterdale. Photographed by Richard Theobald.*

Style

To introduce Jessie Newbery's style, I would like to quote her directly, as reported in *The Studio*. "I believe in education consisting of seeing the best that has been done. Then, having this high standard set before us, in doing what we like to do: *that* for our fathers, *this* for us. I believe that nothing is common or unclean: that the design and decoration of a pepper pot is as important, in its degree, as the conception of a cathedral. ... To descend to particulars, I like opposition of straight lines to curved; of horizontal to vertical; of purple to green; of green to blue. ... I specially aim at beautifully shaped spaces and try to make them as important as the patterns. I try to make most appearance with least effort, but insist that what work is ventured on is as perfect as may be."

The lighter, fresher designs she pioneered represented a change from the heavily ornamented, dense type of art needlework. It was modern and novel. The designs were also lighter and fresher in their colors and their materials. The typical heavy and dark Arts and Crafts blues, greens, and reds turned to pink, pastel blue, lavender, and white in the Glasgow Style. The medium used for the embroidery was usually linen, rather than the heavy wools often favored in art needlework. Jessie Newbery believed strongly that people of all social and economic classes should be able to decorate their soft furnishings and clothing with embroidery, so the materials chosen were deliberately inexpensive.

Mottoes were included as part of the design using the rectilinear Glasgow lettering (see Figure 153). Often, a linear frame is used to anchor the scheme, often with little Glasgow squares.

An important part of Jessie Newbery's work was appliqué. Mrs. Newbery typically sewed the appliqués on using satin stitch; her appliquéd circles of pink linen, with simple lines indicating petal outlines, gave rise to the Glasgow rose. Mrs. Newbery also liked cutwork.

An interesting feature of many Glasgow pieces is the hemming, which is given a decorative finish (see Figures 154 and 156). Sometimes on more elaborate pieces cutwork or drawn threadwork was employed.

Simple stitches were used: satin stitch, long-and-short, French knots. The stitches used were fairly easy, but presented a beautiful effect. No techniques to frighten off beginners were used. Ann Macbeth wrote in her 1920 introduction to *An Embroidery Book* by Anne Knox Arthur, who succeeded her as head of embroidery at the School of Art: "There really is no mystery about stitches; they are but the letters of the needleworker's alphabet, and the words of her language—to be used according to her own ideas. One may embroider poems; another may embroider prayers and praises for her church; another may beautify a fair woman's garment or sing a little song in stitches for a baby's robe..."

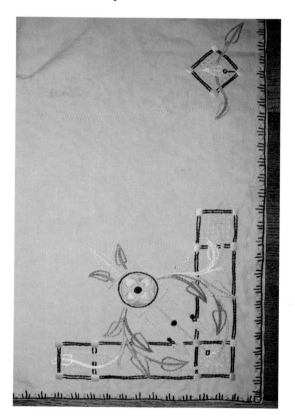

Figure 154. Linen table square with cotton perle embroidery.

Figure 153. Embroidered linen hanging with drawn needlework by unknown artist.

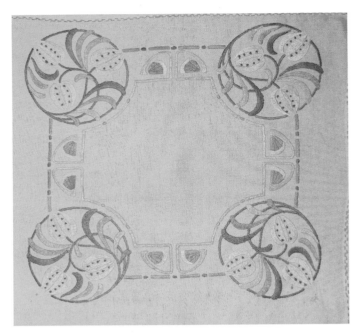

Figure 155. Linen table square with silk embroidery. Probably worked by a Glasgow School of Art Saturday classes student.

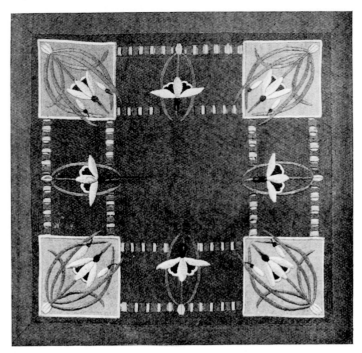

Figure 157. Linen table square with appliqué and embroidery by Ann Macbeth. *The Studio Yearbook 1906.*

Figure 156. Embroidery by Ann Macbeth.
The Studio Yearbook 1906.

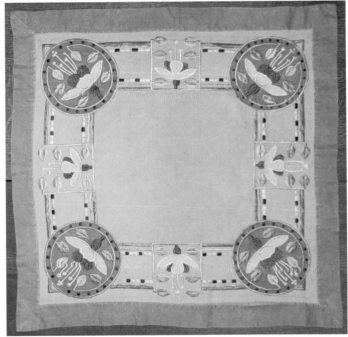

Figure 158. Linen table square with appliqué and embroidery by Ann Macbeth.

Some of Ann Macbeth's earlier work is linen table squares, with floral motifs on the corners (see Figures 156 through 159). She also designed a number of beautiful cushions (see Figure 160) and a portière (see Figure 161). When Miss Macbeth retired to Patterdale in Cumbria, she created a number of beautiful panels for her local church, St Patrick's (see Figure 152).

Figure 159. Linen table square with appliqué and drawn threadwork by Ann Macbeth. *The Studio Volume 24.*

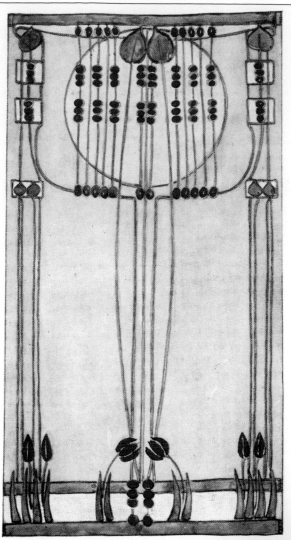

Figure 161. Embroidery design by Ann Macbeth, *Educational Needlecraft*. Longmans, Green and Co. 1913.

Figure 160. Embroidery by Ann Macbeth. *The Studio Yearbook 1906*

That motto in thc same lettering appears on a room screen (see Figures 162 and 163) known to have been embroidered by Gertrude Anderson. Since Miss Anderson is recorded in *The Studio* as having executed another of Miss Macbeth's designs, the screen is also attributed to Miss Macbeth's design.

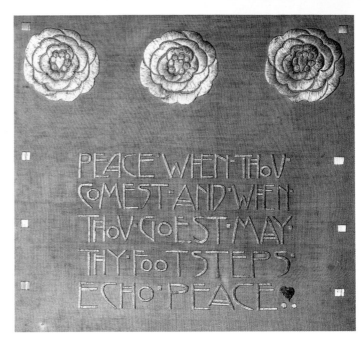

Figure 162. Panel from a three-panel room screen, linen with silk thread, embroidered by Gertrude Anderson, design attributed to Ann Macbeth.

Later, Miss Macbeth started using decorative figural panels on silk satin (see Figures 164 and 165). She considered that this fabric, while luxurious, gave the best background. Miss Macbeth believed that figures represented "the highest and most difficult achievement of the craft."

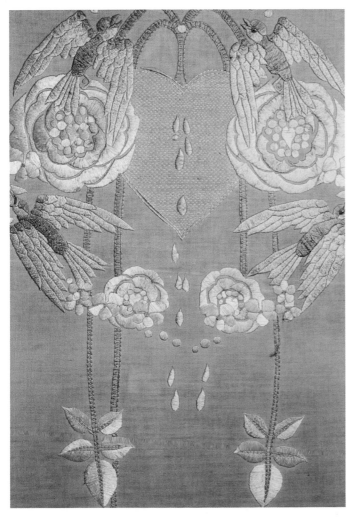

Figure 163. Panel from a three-panel room screen, linen with silk thread, embroidered by Gertrude Anderson, design attributed to Ann Macbeth.

Figure 164. *Saint Margaret*, a figural panel designed and worked by Ann Macbeth. *The Studio Yearbook 1912.*

Figure 165. *Saint Elizabeth*, a figural panel designed by Ann Macbeth. Silk thread on silk background with pearl and wirework inclusions. *Courtesy Woolley & Wallis.*

Figure 166 is a figural altar panel by Ann Macbeth, and Figures 167 and 168 show figure panels designed by various other Glasgow students. Helen Lamb studied at the Glasgow School of Art, where she produced the piece in Figure 167. It's a charming work, filled with the roses that signal femininity and feminism in the Glasgow Style. Through the roses on her dress to the roses in her hand, the girl becomes a part of the rose bower. Helen Lamb's work in different media can be seen today in Dunblane Cathedral.

Figure 166. Pulpit fall designed by Ann Macbeth. *The Studio Yearbook 1911.*

Figure 167. Figural panel by Helen Lamb. *The Studio Yearbook 1910.*

Figure 168. Figural panel by Rachel George. *The Studio Yearbook 1908.*

Two other Glasgow students designed the work in Figures 169 and 170. An English artist who produced Glasgow Style embroidery while studying in Liverpool under Frances Macdonald McNair (one of the Glasgow Four, along with her husband, Charles Rennie Mackintosh and Margaret Macdonald Mackintosh) was Mary "Bee" Phillips, for whose wedding present Herbert McNair created a pair of silver tongs with a bee motif. She designed the bird panel in Figure 171.

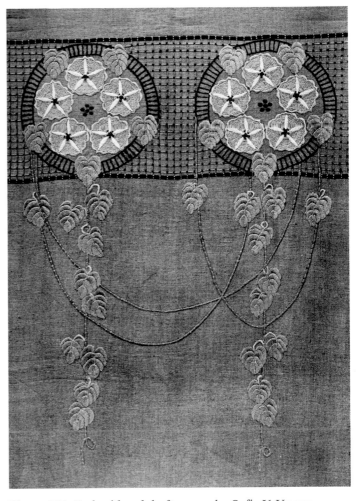

Figure 170. Embroidered draft screen by Sofia Y. Young. *The Studio Volume 51.*

Figure 169. Cushion by Milly Morgan. *The Studio Yearbook 1911.*

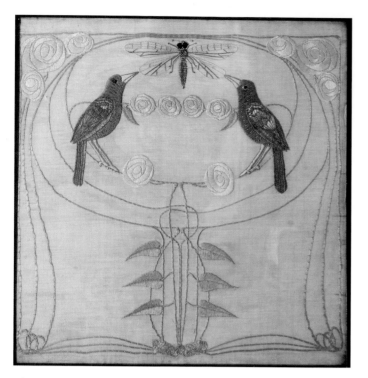

Figure 172. Embroidered silk panel worked by Elise Prioleau and probably designed by Jessie M. King. © *Christie's Images Ltd.*

Figure 171. Embroidered panel by Mary Phillips, silk on linen with glass beads.

The great Glasgow illustrator Jessie M. King collaborated with French master embroiderer Elise Prioleau to create needlework pictures based on Miss King's pictures (see Figures 172 and 173). Miss King's best friend, Helen Paxton Brown, was renowned for her embroidery (see Figure 174).

Figure 173. Embroidered silk panel worked by Elise Prioleau and designed by Jessie M. King. *The Studio Volume 51.*

Figure 174. Embroideries by Helen Paxton Brown (upper) and Rhoda Wager (lower). *The Studio Volume 50.*

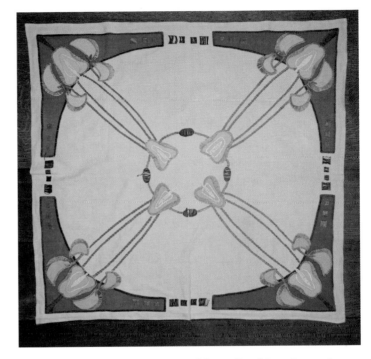

Figure 175. Linen table square with appliquéd apples and embroidery by Mary Hogg.

In 1907 Mary Hogg was awarded a scholarship to evening classes at the Glasgow School (see Figure 175). Until her marriage in 1917, she worked as an embroidery teacher at the School and exhibited at the Lady Artists' Club.

Johnamm "Joe" McCrae attended the Glasgow School of Art starting in 1898, and won many prizes for drawing, design, and painting. She won a £5 bursary in 1902 and, with it, visited London art galleries and museums. She became a teacher at the School in 1906 but had to retire shortly afterward to care for her nieces after her sister's death. Figure 176 was embroidered by her.

Rhoda Wager was born in 1875 at Mile End Old Town, London. She studied drawing, painting, and embroidery at the Glasgow School of Art from 1897 to 1903 (see Figure 174, lower piece). She exhibited widely, and was a member of the Glasgow Society of Lady Artists. She was taught to make jewelry by Bernard Cuzner, a silversmith best known today for designing some of Liberty's Cymric and Tudric metalwork. In 1913, Miss Wager went to live on her brother's sugar plantation in Fiji. Moving to Australia in 1918, she began making jewelry in Sydney and is remembered today for her Arts and Crafts jewelry.

Figure 176. Embroidered, appliquéd cushion by Joe McCrae. *The Art Journal, 1907.*

Of course, much Glasgow Style embroidery cannot be attributed to any known maker, but it's still a joy to look at (see Figures 177 through 185). In 1900, the Scottish Education Department decided that embroidery was an important part of a girl's education; needlework became a required subject for teachers in Scotland. Therefore, the Glasgow School set up Saturday classes for teachers to improve their design and embroidery skills. After three years of study, the teachers received certification from the Scottish Education Department. Figure 186 is a lovely embroidery by Mary Begg, a teacher in Motherwell who was known for her embroidery and probably attended the Saturday classes.

Jessie Newbery started the classes, and then charged Ann Macbeth with managing them. Miss Macbeth developed new methods of teaching sewing and embroidery to children. While previously children were started on hemming and pointless samplers, under Miss Macbeth's tutelage, each lesson, from the first, resulted in a finished piece for the child. The child's skills were developed via lessons appropriate to varying age levels. For example, younger, more nearsighted children were given more coarse work, usually using colored threads on light backgrounds to make the stitching easier to see. (The white-on-white stitching usually taught was considered by Miss Macbeth to be bad for the children's eyesight.)

Other lessons aimed to develop the child's creativity, the idea being that the design should derive from the technique employed.

Ann Macbeth in *An Embroidery Book*: "Some of the most interesting embroideries done during the last few years have been planned and carried out by our Scottish schools by untrained workers—designs so simple that the workers do not realize they are designing at all—since they draw largely with needle and thread alone and have little assistance from chalk and other markings. And it is this type of work, usually sewn in coarse yarns and on rough canvas, flannel, or homespun, that is perhaps the most happy and most stimulating for a designer of needlework to begin on. The work is so quickly achieved—so gallant and bright in color—so utilitarian in purpose and of so little cost in outlay, that is above all others to be recommended."

It's my opinion that Glasgow Style embroidery is the finest the Arts and Crafts Movement produced. The work is fresh and original—not historically derivative—most of the artists designed and executed their own pieces, and, unlike most of the rest of the Arts and Crafts Movement, the embroidery was usually valued as much as other forms of art. At its best, Glasgow Style embroidery is a fine art, not a decorative art.

Figure 177. Embroidered and appliqué bags and table covers by Glasgow School students. *The Studio Volume 27.*

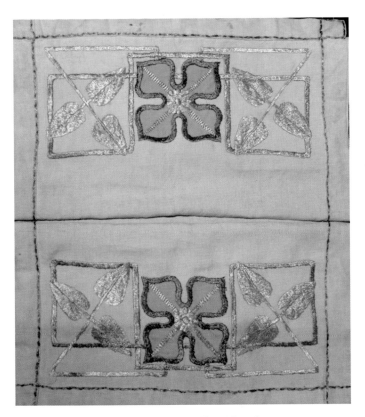

Figure 178. Linen runner with appliquéd and silk embroidered blue clematis.

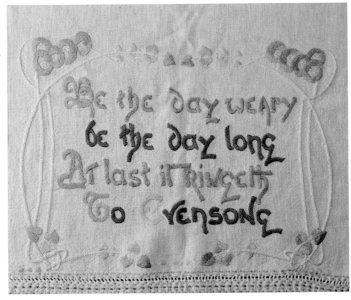

Figure 179. Chair back of coarse linen with silk embroidered motto.

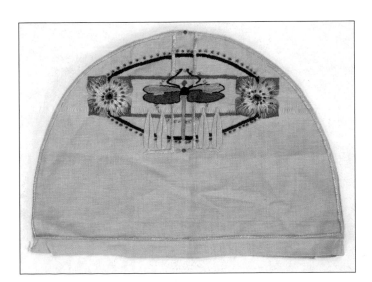

Figure 180. Tea cozy, embroidered linen with dragonfly design. *Courtesy of Liberty & Co.*

Figure 181. White rose embroidered hanging, silk thread on linen. *Courtesy of Liberty & Co.*

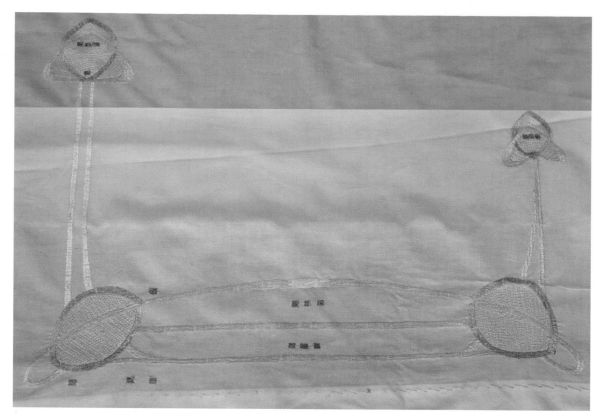

Figure 182. Single curtain, silk, with silk embroidery in "outer space" design.

Figure 183. Cushion cover with embroidered rose and geometric motif. *Courtesy of the Millinery Works, photographed by Jefferson Smith.*

Figure 184. A framed embroidered panel in silk on linen with cutwork birds and roses. *Courtesy of the Millinery Works, photographed by Jefferson Smith.*

Figure 185. Glasgow Style embroidered panel, worked as a pair of birds perched on a stylized flowering tree reserved on a blue woven cotton ground. *Courtesy of Lyon & Turnbull.*

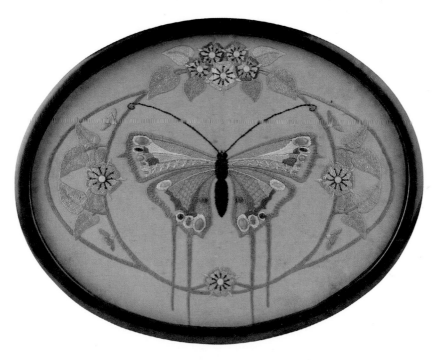

Figure 186. Butterfly embroidery worked in colored silks with applied beads, by Mary Begg. *Courtesy of Lyon & Turnbull.*

Chapter 7

Candace Wheeler

One middle-aged lady saw the works exhibited by the Royal School of Art Needlework at the Centennial Exposition in Philadelphia and was inspired. In 1876, forty-nine-year-old Candace Wheeler was the energetic wife of a wealthy New York merchant and mother of four. (Figure 187 shows Mrs. Wheeler in later life painted by her daughter Dora.) She was an amateur painter and friend to many New York artists and designers. But through her own powerful personality and indefatigable energy, Wheeler forged an important career in textiles, embroidery, and interior design.

Mrs. Wheeler was a feminist of a charitable bent. In the 1870s there were many widows and unmarried women who were social and economic casualties of the Civil War; how could such women make their living? How could any lady who needed to earn her living do so with dignity? Before the Industrial Revolution, women could make their living doing home-based work such as sewing, baking, or weaving, but these were no longer practicable.

Sarah Bolton wrote in *Wide Awake* (1887), "Mrs. Wheeler sat down at her desk and wrote a circular and printed it at her own expense, telling the women of New York that it was proposed to form a large and influential association for the purpose of establishing a place for the exhibition and sale of 'sculptures, paintings, wood-carvings, paintings upon slate, porcelain and pottery, art and ecclesiastical needle-work, tapestry and hangings,' which work shall be done by women." This became the Society of Decorative Arts, a school, workshop, exhibition gallery, and sales outlet devoted to training female artists and craftspeople. Mrs. Wheeler also helped to start similar societies in cities across the United States. Figure 188 shows scenes from the SDA printed in *Harper's Bazar*, May 28, 1881. Figures 189 through 192 show sample work from the Society of Decorative Arts. It would be nice to say that the society produced high quality art needlework in line with the RSAN, but judging from the pictures from *The Art Journal*, the standard was average Victorian.

Figure 187. Candace Wheeler, painted by Dora Wheeler. *The Development of Embroidery in America.*

Figure 188. Scenes from the Society of Decorative Arts. *Harper's Bazaar,* May 28, 1881

Figure 189. Embroidery work from the New York Society of Decorative Art. *The Art Journal Volume 4, 1878.*

Figure 190. Embroidery work from the New York Society of Decorative Art. *The Art Journal Volume 4, 1878.*

Figure 191. Embroidery work from the New York Society of Decorative Art. *The Art Journal Volume 4, 1878.*

Figure 192. Embroidery work from the New York Society of Decorative Art. *The Art Journal Volume 4, 1878.*

Figure 193. Embroidery of madonna lilies, wool twill embroidered with wool and silk thread, silk velvet border. *Image copyright © The Metropolitan Museum of Art. Image source: Art Resource, NY.*

In 1878, for ladies whose skills were less artistic and more homelike, Wheeler began the New York Exchange for Women's Work, where women could sell anything handmade, including baked goods, toys, fancywork, and so on. (The New York Exchange continued until 2003, when, sadly, it closed.)

But also at this time, Wheeler needed to earn money herself. Her husband was suffering from depression and his business wasn't earning much; meanwhile, they still had children to provide for. In 1878 she exhibited a textile she designed herself, an embroidered mantle shelf decoration, and soon became known as a talented embroiderer and designer in her own right. The pillow cover shown in

Figure 193 is an early work by Wheeler from about this time. The crewelwork lilies are very similar to those on a curtain exhibited by the Royal School of Art Needlework at the Centennial Exposition.

One of the teachers at the Society of Decorative Art was Louis Comfort Tiffany, whose father had founded the jewelry company. In 1879, Tiffany and Mrs. Wheeler formed a decorating firm, which eventually became known as Associated Artists. By 1883, there were four artists: Lockwood de Forest and Samuel Colman had joined. Each was in charge of his or her own sphere; Mrs. Wheeler's was textiles and embroidery.

The firm was quite successful, becoming famous for using native American species of flowers and plants, especially ivy, lilies, and pine cones. It decorated a number of important interiors; the Veterans' Room of the Seventh Regiment Armory is still partially intact. Figure 194 shows the room as it was; sadly not in color as the company was famous for its skillful use of color. Unfortunately I have been unable to find an image of the hangings done by Mrs. Wheeler, but they were described to us by Constance Cary Harrison in *Woman's Handiwork in Modern Homes* (1881): "The four plush window-curtains for the Veterans' Room at the Armory are made two of Damascus red, two of antique blue. A network of gilded leather is embroidered upon the plush, leaving flame-shaped interstices like the slashings of an ancient doublet. The portière is of Japanese brocade, bordered with plush representing leopard skin. Upon the main body of the portière are laid appliqués of velvet in small squares, each exhibiting a design taken from the days of knighthood and romantic warfare. Over the intermediate spaces of brocade are sewn tiny rings of steel, representing the surface of a coat of mail."

It's unfortunate that embroidery and textiles in general are the most fugitive of the decorative arts. I'd love to see this Associated Artists piece, also described in the book: "... a portière designed to accord with an interior suggesting the suburbs of storied Granada rather than modern Fifth Avenue. This sumptuous hanging, made of opalescent plushes, is, like the moonstone, full of imprisoned light. A mass of fine embroidery, in gold and silk, surrounds underlet disks of satin containing old Greek needle-work incorporated into the stuff by many skilful stitches. The whole is a feast of fleeting color—whether rose or azure, cream or gold, the eye fails to decide."

Associated Artists redecorated the White House after President James A. Garfield's assassination. Chester A. Arthur refused to move in until it had been redecorated. (President Garfield lay ill in the White House for two months after being shot.)

Another Associated Artists-designed interior was Mark Twain's house in Hartford, Connecticut, which has recently been restored as much as possible. The firm also decorated the drawing room of the fabulous mansion of Cornelius Vanderbilt II (now sadly demolished), as well as the George Kemp house, often considered L.C. Tiffany's finest decorating achievement. The squash- and eggplant-patterned stained glass windows from the Kemp house still exist in a museum in Orlando, Florida.

Figure 194. Veterans' Room of the Seventh Regiment Armory. *Bain News Service, Library of Congress.*

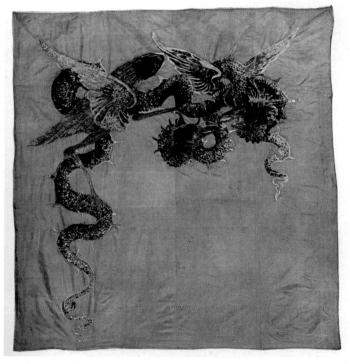

Figure 195. *Fighting Dragons*, embroidery designed by Candace Wheeler, worked by Associated Artists. *The Development of Embroidery in America.*

Another gorgeous item, now lost, was a curtain for the old Madison Square Theater. Mrs. Wheeler described it in her book *The Development of Embroidery in America* (1921): "The design for this curtain turned out to be a very realistic view of a vista in the woods, which gave opportunity for wonderful studies of color, from clear sunlit foregrounds to tangles of misty green, melting into blue perspectives of distance. It was really a daring experiment in methods of appliqué, for no stitchery pure and simple was in place in the wide reaches of the picture. So we went on painting a woods interior in materials of all sorts, from tenuous crepes to solid velvets and plushes. … I remember the great delight in marking the difference between oak and birch trees and fitting each with its appropriate effect of color and texture of leaf; and the building of a tall gray-green yucca, with its thick satin leaves and tall white pyramidal groups of velvet blossoms, standing in the very foreground, was as exciting as if it were standing posed for its portrait, and being painted in oils." The piece was set on fire by a careless workman one year after it was installed in the theater. Sigh.

In 1883, the firm of Associated Artists dissolved. The partners wanted to pursue work in their individual fields by themselves. Mrs. Wheeler wanted to concentrate on textile design rather than decorating. At the age of 56, Wheeler then founded her own textile firm called, confusingly, Associated Artists. Figure 195 shows a textile from Associated Artists II called *Fighting Dragons*, made in 1885.

Another textile, circa 1883-87, demonstrates the fabulous effects Wheeler could get with appliqué and embroidery, even though it is not in the best condition (see Figure 196). Wheeler liked using appliqué along with embroidery because it was a speedier and cheaper way to produce a large textile (as with the theater curtain above). This piece is unfinished but was almost certainly meant to be the center of a portière or curtain. The ground fabric is cloth-of-gold by the Cheney Brothers mill, one of the first silk mills in America (you'll read about the American silk industry in the next chapter). The tulips are pink silk velvet, while the stems and edges of the leaves are couched with metallic threads.

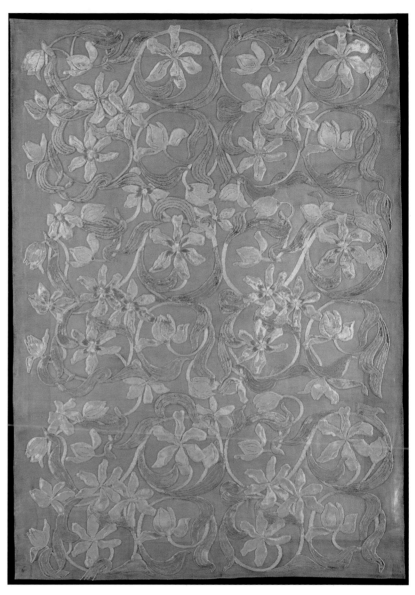

Figure 196. Tulips embroidery: silk and metallic cloth appliquéd with silk velvet and embroidered with silk and metallic-wrapped cotton threads. *Image copyright © The Metropolitan Museum of Art. Image source: Art Resource, NY.*

The work in Figure 197, which is known as *Penelope Unraveling Her Work at Night*, is the only known example of a process patented by Candace Wheeler known as needlewoven tapestry. In this process, a heavy woven silk canvas is used as the base cloth and then stitches are passed through the warp or weft with a needle. It gives the appearance of tapestry but it's really embroidery. This work was drawn by Dora Wheeler, Candace's daughter, who studied art in Paris. She designed many of these needlewoven tapestries with female figures on them, including Minnehaha and other characters from literature; they were popular owing to the rich effect they gave with shimmering metallic threads. This piece was given to Mrs. Wheeler's granddaughter; it eventually made its way to the Shelburne Museum in Vermont where it lay unknown until it was rediscovered just prior to the 2001 retrospective on Mrs. Wheeler's work.

Associated Artists II continued until 1907, although Mrs. Wheeler herself stopped working at the firm in 1900. She retired but she started writing books on interior design; her most well-known book was *The Development of Embroidery in America*, published in 1921. She died in 1923. Dora Wheeler Keith donated a number of her mother's works to the Metropolitan Museum, which were accepted even though they were considered hopelessly old-fashioned. This may well have saved them, because they were stored safely for many years. The Metropolitan Museum is now virtually the only institution in the world to have examples of Candace Wheeler's work. She was given her first full exhibition in 2001 with "Candace Wheeler: The Art and Enterprise of American Design, 1875-1900," curated by Amelia Peck.

Candace Wheeler was a pioneer, showing that middle class women could sustain their families through decorative arts, even in middle age, when most Victorian women would be considered elderly.

Figure 197. *Penelope Unraveling Her Work at Night*, needle woven tapestry by Dora Wheeler. *Image copyright © The Metropolitan Museum of Art. Image source: Art Resource, NY.*

Chapter 8

American Arts and Crafts Embroidery

In 1897, a group of architects, educators, craftspeople, and collectors interested in the British Arts and Crafts Movement met at the Museum of Fine Arts, Boston, to organize a similar kind of applied arts exhibition in America. The first American Arts and Crafts Exhibition opened on April 5, 1897, at Copley Hall. This exhibition was very successful, so its organizers incorporated as the Society of Arts and Crafts three months later. (The Society of Arts and Crafts still sponsors contemporary crafts shows in Boston.)

The mission statement of the SAC was as follows: "This Society was incorporated for the purpose of promoting artistic work in all branches of handicraft. It hopes to bring Designers and Workmen into mutually helpful relations, and to encourage workmen to execute designs of their own. It endeavors to stimulate in workmen an appreciation of the dignity and value of good design; to counteract the popular impatience of Law and Form, and the desire for over-ornamentation and specious originality. It will insist upon the necessity of sobriety and restraint, or ordered arrangement, of due regard for the relation between the form of an object and its use, and of harmony and fitness in the decoration put upon it."

These ideas rippled through the world of American design. One person who noticed was a man called Gustav Stickley.

Gustav Stickley

Gustav Stickley (see Figure 198) was born in Osceola, Wisconsin, in 1858. He was the first son in a family of nine children; he and his four brothers all became furniture makers. At the age of eighteen, Stickley was apprenticed to his uncle's furniture factory in Pennsylvania. In 1883, he and brothers Charles and Albert formed a furniture company called Stickley Brothers, but in 1888, Stickley formed another company with a new partner. Ten years later, becoming interested in the nascent Arts and Crafts movement, Stickley bought out his partner and struck out on his own, creating the Gustav Stickley Company in Syracuse, New York.

Stickley took trips to England and read magazines like *The Studio*; clearly there were new, interesting ideas about design to explore and untapped markets. The United States population was growing rapidly and becoming more urban. Yet concerns about health and cleanliness made Americans yearn for the simple, pure country life. Simpler, plainer country furniture seemed to suit the mood.

Figure 198. Gustav Stickley, father of the American Arts and Crafts Movement.

In 1900, Stickley's first Arts and Crafts furniture was produced—mostly plain, simple pieces, but exquisitely designed and meticulously crafted. In 1901, Stickley founded a periodical, *The Craftsman*, an outlet for Stickley's own ideals—although the text was written by others—which served as an advertisement for Stickley's product line, now called United Crafts and expanded to metalware, leather goods, and so on. Significantly, the first issue of *The Craftsman* was dedicated to William Morris. Over the life of the publication, *The Craftsman* not only promoted Stickley's business but also brought the latest design ideas from Europe to the American public.

Textiles were an important part of Stickley's business, and were instrumental in softening the severe lines of the furniture. Stickley's are some of the first true American Arts and Crafts embroideries that exist. You could buy the needlework already done or order stamped materials and floss to work it yourself at home.

The August 1903 issue of *The Craftsman* printed eight designs for portières designed by Harvey Ellis and Claude Bragdon (see Figure 199). Portières one, four, and six are extremely Glasgow in design, while number eight recalls Voysey.

Many Stickley designs were more stylized and plain than these, though. An early Craftsman catalog, c. 1905, explains, "The Craftsman method of decorating textiles is exceedingly simple, the object being to obtain good lines and broad effects in color and mass, without too much detail. Therefore, many of our designs are carried out by means of the appliqué of one fabric upon another, needlework being used only for outlines and for additional touches of decoration." The *Teazle* design shown in Figure 200, a stylized version of a plant similar to the thistle, is appliquéd, as is the *Lotus* runner in Figure 201.

Figure 202 shows a *China Tree* runner; the needlework is done in a darning stitch that became popular for embroidery. Darned work was used "where simple forms and broad masses of solid colors do not seem desirable … This form of needlework is especially interesting, as it gives the effect of being so thoroughly identified with the fabric as almost to have been woven in …"

The Stickley catalog says, "Both in form and workmanship this design is simplicity itself. It is darned in light leaf green linen floss, the threads running straight across with the woof. The outlines

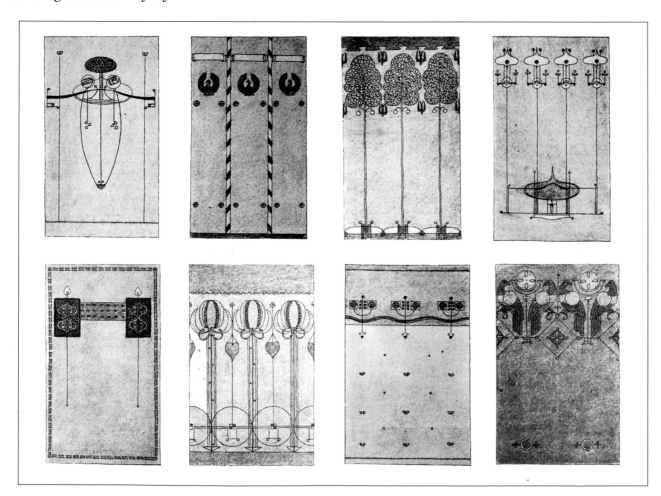

Figure 199. Portière designs by Harvey Ellis and Claude Bragdon. *The Craftsman*, August 1903.

of the trees and branches are afterwards picked out with a tiny broken thread of dark blue, simply run in stitches of short uneven lengths around the edges. It is the merest hint of an edge of color which brings out the tree forms without the sharp decisiveness given by the outline stitch." (Unfortunately this example is sadly faded.)

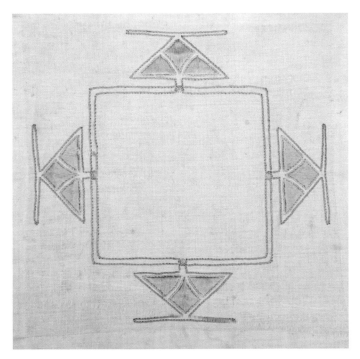

Figure 200. *Teazle* design runner by Craftsman Workshops, linen appliquéd with linen thread. *Collection of Jessica Greenway.*

Figure 201. *Lotus* design runner by Craftsman Workshops, linen appliquéd with linen thread. *Collection of Jessica Greenway.*

Figure 202. *China Tree* linen table scarf, Craftsman #918. *Courtesy Treadway Gallery.*

Less faded, happily, is the *Magnolia* table scarf in Figure 203, which also uses the darned stitch. Confusingly, Stickley sold three different magnolia designs: this one (*Magnolia*), *Japanese Magnolia*, and *Conventionalized Magnolia* (see Figure 204). *Magnolia* and *Conventionalized Magnolia* are later designs than *Japanese Magnolia*; the latter from the earlier catalog and the former from the 1912 catalog. My favorite Stickley design is *Horse Chestnut*, in Figure 205. The stylized trees with giant chestnuts are extremely appealing.

So what happened to Stickley? Unfortunately, he overextended himself and the company right before the First World War and just as fashions were changing. His brothers' company survived, but his did not. He died in obscurity, but was rediscovered starting in the 1970s. Now his work commands extremely high prices and he is considered the father of the American Arts and Crafts Movement.

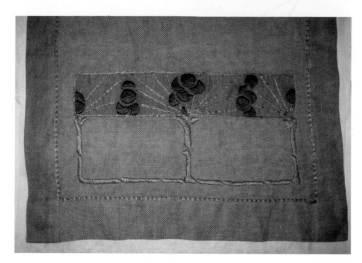

Figure 205. *Horse Chestnut* table scarf by Craftsman Workshops. *Collection of Timothy Hansen and Dianne Ayres.*

American Design

American Arts and Crafts embroidery differs from British designs in color, form, and design. Part of the reason for this is that the American Arts and Crafts movement was most popular after the British designs began to fade from popularity. For example, geometric forms introduced by Viennese designers are popular motifs in American Arts and Crafts textiles. The black outlines of these pieces can also be attributed to the Viennese influence, although black outlines can also hide mediocre satin stitching.

The colors used in American embroidery—rich golds, greens, reds, browns—harmonize with the colors used in the Craftsman or bungalow style of decorating that was beginning to be popular around the turn of the century. Textiles were, however, important parts of a bungalow interior. Hard furniture needed cushions for comfort; portières were needed to exclude drafts (as were heavy curtains), and the curtains and table squares or runners brighten the often-austere bungalow interiors.

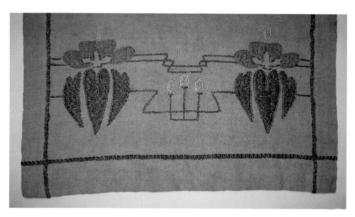

Figure 203. *Magnolia* table scarf with darned stitching. *Collection of Timothy Hansen and Dianne Ayres.*

The women's magazines of the time included patterns and designs in the Arts and Crafts style. Popular titles such as *Modern Priscilla, Home Needlework*, and *Needlecraft* did much to promulgate the new look. In these magazines, everything could be embroidered, no matter how pointless: beach pillows (mmm, sandy); lettuce bags (you don't keep your lettuce in a bag?); cravat holders; whisk broom holders; pin cushions; shaving paper pads (for putting on cuts); hair receivers (these days we use something we call the trash); and bags for rubbers (mind out of the gutter). Figure 206 shows a bag for storing your galoshes in between wearings. (Why did people keep their old hair? Either for stuffing pillows or pincushions or for making rats. What's a rat? A hair pad. You wanted your Gibson Girl pompadour as high and full as possible.)

Figure 204. *Conventionalized Magnolia* table scarf by Craftsman Workshops. *Collection of Timothy Hansen and Dianne Ayres.*

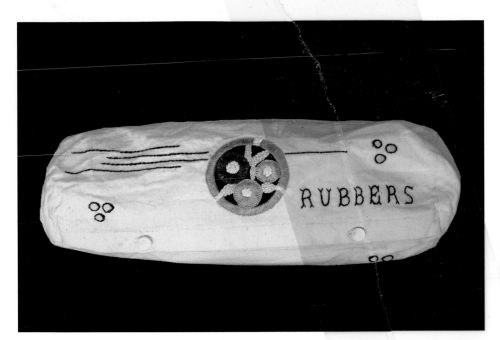

Figure 206. Embroidered linen galoshes bag.

Figure 207. Embroidered bags for storing cutlery, with original 50¢ price tag attached. *Collection of Kim Covey*.

Figure 208. Linen collars and cuffs bag. *Collection of L. Teresa Di Biase*.

Bags, embroidered bags of course, were needed for everything from cutlery (see Figure 207), collars and cuffs (see Figure 208), laundry (Figure 209), slippers (Figure 210), men's celluloid collars (Figure 211), or just for general bagging (see Figures 212 through 222). Some of the "general" bags shown here would have been made to hold your needlework, while others were used as handbags. Figures 213 and 215 were probably made by Royal Society, while the gold bag in Figure 220 features "Wallachian" embroidery, where small celluloid discs were applied to the surface of the fabric and then covered with stitches.

Figure 209. Linen laundry bag. *Collection of Kim Covey.*

Figure 210. Linen slippers bag. *Collection of Kim Covey.*

Figure 211. Linen bag for collars. *Collection of Jessica Greenway.*

Figure 212. Embroidered linen bag. *Collection of Kim Covey.*

Figure 213. Embroidered linen bag. *Collection of Jessica Greenway.*

Figure 214. Embroidered linen bag. *Collection of Jane Roe.*

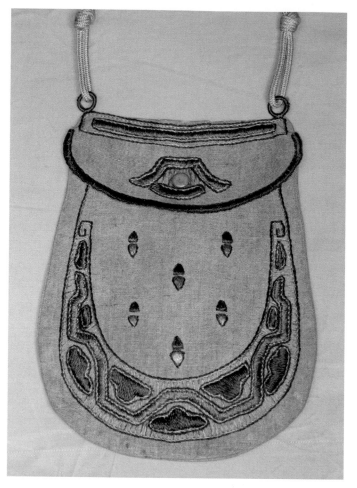

Figure 215. Embroidered linen bag. *Collection of Jane Roe.*

Figure 216. Embroidered linen bag. *Collection of Jane Roe.*

Figure 217. Embroidered linen bag. *Collection of Lorrie Moore.*

Figure 218. Embroidered linen bag. *Collection of Lorrie Moore.*

Figure 219. Embroidered linen bag (cord not original). *Collection of Lorrie Moore.*

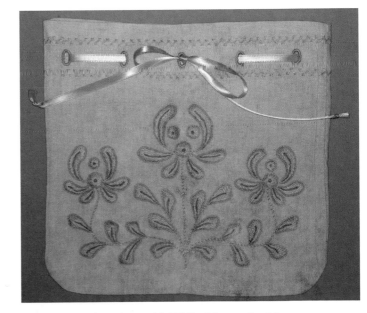

Figure 220. Linen bag with Wallachian embroidery. *Collection of Lorrie Moore.*

Figure 221. Embroidered linen bag.
Collection of L. Teresa Di Biase.

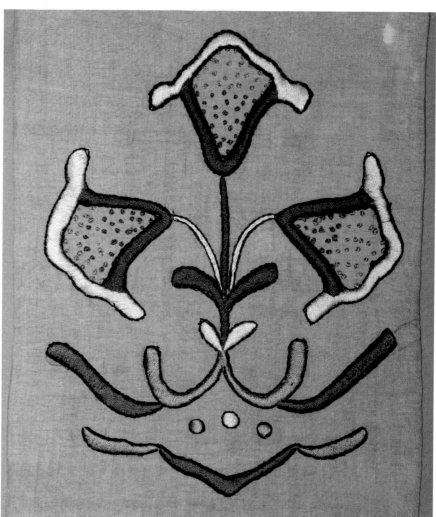

Figure 222. Embroidered linen bag.
Collection of Lorric Moore.

Deerfield Society of Blue and White

The Deerfield Society of Blue and White Needlework was founded in 1896. Margaret Whiting (1860-1946) and Ellen Miller (1854-1929) became interested in the American colonial embroidery they found in the museum in Deerfield, Massachusetts. They thought the design and workmanship of the old embroideries were far superior to modern versions, but the old work was moth-eaten and half-forgotten, so they formed an organization to promote it.

The women also decided to reproduce the antique embroideries and offer them for sale. They experimented with vegetable dyes to replicate the old work exactly. Local women, as many as thirty at a time, were paid 20¢ an hour to embroider, sew, and make baskets (see Figure 223). Portières, tablecloths, wall hangings, antimacassars, as well as baskets for sale were displayed in the front parlor of the Miller home.

The New York Evening Post reported in 1897, "The Deerfield Society of Blue and White Needlework is in perfect harmony with its environment: it is colonial and puritan, it is artistic, it is loyal to its traditions, patriotic, and there is not another like it."

Figure 223. Deerfield women embroidering. *The Craftsman*, November 1903.

Eventually the Deerfield Society offered original works for sale in colors other than blue and white. Figures 224 and 225 show such a design. Notice the Society's emblem in Figure 226, a D inside a spinning wheel. Only the best work was allowed to be marked this way.

The Society of Blue and White was so successful that it inspired others in the town of Deerfield to embrace the Arts and Crafts Movement. *The New York Times* wrote in 1905, "Once a year there is a pilgrimage of lovers of beautiful handiwork to Deerfield, Mass., to worship at the shrine of the Deerfield Arts and Crafts Society. Every Summer the busy workers of the town put their handicraft on view, and then stand back out of sight while visitors admire and praise."

The Society remained a thriving woman-owned business until the aging partners decided to disband it in 1926. While many of their designs are not necessarily what we would think of as Arts and Crafts, the Society was an important part of the movement.

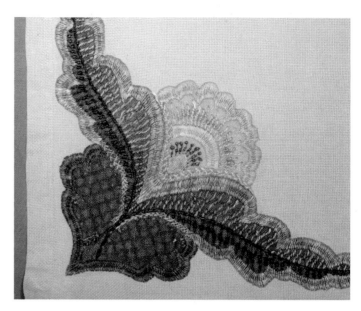

Figure 225. Close up of Deerfield Society table center. *Collection of Lorrie Moore.*

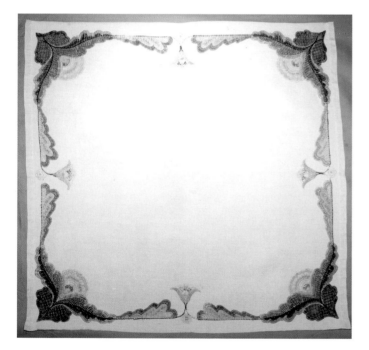

Figure 224. Deerfield Society table center, linen embroidered and appliquéd. *Collection of Lorrie Moore.*

Figure 226. Deerfield Society mark. *Collection of Lorrie Moore.*

Newcomb

Newcomb College was a women's college attached to Tulane University. (It was merged in 2006 into the other undergraduate colleges at Tulane.)

Newcomb was founded by Josephine Louise Newcomb in 1886 in memory of her daughter, Sophie, who died aged fifteen years. Newcomb's art school taught crafts in accordance with the progressive spirit of the Arts and Crafts Movement, and also to ensure that the young women had practical skills for earning a living, which was important in the economically devastated postwar South. The best known Newcomb craft is pottery; the pottery's first head was Mary Given Sheerer, who had worked at Rookwood.

Newcomb was also acclaimed for its embroidery department, founded in 1901. *The Craftsman* wrote in 1903, "It is upon the excellence of design that Newcomb especially builds its school of needlework. It recognizes that nature alone initiates. It asks that ornament be more than an aggregation of conventional forms; that it represent the ego of the period in which it is created, as well as that of the creator. A satisfactory result presupposes sane and intelligent discrimination among wide traditions, and ability to adapt those natural forms which loving and intimate association have made most familiar, to materials which combine use and beauty." Figure 227 shows a piece attributed to Newcomb. Pieces of Newcomb embroidery are extremely rare today.

The work in Figure 227 shows the influence of Arthur Wesley Dow on American Arts and Crafts design. Arthur Wesley Dow (1857-1922) was a prolific painter, printmaker, photographer, and arts teacher. He influenced generations of artists, including Georgia O'Keeffe, Charles Sheeler, Edward Steichen, and Alfred Stieglitz.

Dow's 1899 book *Composition: A Series of Exercises in Art Structure for the Use of Students and Teachers* changed the teaching of art in America. His ideas played a pivotal role in the American Arts and Crafts Movement. He believed that artists should design based on elements of composition, like line, mass, and color, rather than direct imitation of nature (over to you, Henry Cole). He himself was profoundly influenced by Japanese woodblock prints. His summer art school in Ipswich, Massachusetts, was attended by artists from Newcomb College.

At Newcomb College, the true Arts and Crafts ideal was followed: one single craftsperson to design and make each piece from start to finish. But most American women were too busy or not interested in designing their own embroidery. They preferred to embroider following a pattern or through a kit. American needleworkers generally saw themselves as consumers rather than designers. Fortunately, there was a large industry ready to provide them with designs.

Figure 227. Embroidered linen panel attributed to Newcomb College. *Collection of Timothy Hansen and Dianne Ayres.*

From Moth to Cloth

From about 1850–1930, the United States silk industry was the largest in the world. To promote their products, large companies produced floss, kits, and books of instructions for needlework. At no time, I must point out, was what we consider Arts and Crafts design today the most popular style in needlework; the best known suppliers that produced Arts and Crafts designs include Corticelli, Royal Society, Brainerd & Armstrong, Belding, and Richardson.

Why was the American silk industry, now gone, so huge? In the early 1830s, there was an economic bubble in mulberry trees, similar to the tech stock bubble of the late 1990s. The idea was that you'd plant some mulberry trees, add some silkworms, and before you knew it you'd be rich.

Silkworms eat only mulberry trees. From the 1770s on, farmers in New England tried to cultivate the mulberry, but the weather made it impossible. But in 1826, a hardier variety of mulberry was introduced. The U.S. House of Representatives in 1826 passed a resolution to issue a report on the economic opportunities of sericulture. The 220–page manual, *Growth and Manufacture of Silk*, urged farmers to grow mulberry trees. This fueled a decade-long economic bubble in mulberry trees. Thousands of people planted acres of mulberry trees; the price of trees rose from $4 per 100 in 1834 to $30 per 100 in 1836. By 1839, when mulberry trees were priced at $500 per 100, the trees were too valuable to be used to feed silkworms.

New England was particularly vulnerable to this fad—since large-scale farming was moving west, any kind of agricultural alternative was eagerly tried. But inevitably the bubble burst. Recurrent fungal blights, cold winters, and the financial Panic of 1837 all brought the silk bubble to an end.

Nonotuck

One speculator, Samuel Whitmarsh, moved to Northampton, Massachusetts, to begin sericulture. He planted mulberry trees and built a cocoonery on the land; a four-story brick factory was built nearby. Unfortunately, the Northampton Silk Company burst with the mulberry bubble in 1840. The bankrupt Whitmarsh cleared out. (Undaunted, Whitmarsh later tried sericulture in Jamaica. That didn't work either. By the time of his death in 1875, Whitmarsh was planning to raise silk in California.)

This scene was replicated across New England. In Connecticut, the Cheney brothers—Ward, Frank, and Rush—had invested heavily in mulberry trees. But when the bubble popped, they were smart enough to realize that even if Americans couldn't grow silk, they could make it into thread. Imported raw silk from China, Europe, and Japan took the place of the native American silk.

Back in Northampton, a man called Samuel Lapham Hill was interested in solving the problem of thread for the newly invented Singer sewing machine. The machine demanded a stronger, smoother filament than had been standard for silk thread used for hand sewing—the machine could not cope with lumps and the thread had to be strong enough not to break under machine tension. He purchased Whitmarsh's mill. In 1855, the Nonotuck Silk Company was formed; the brand name for Hill's "machine twist" was named Corticelli, to sound Italian. This thread was celebrated at the Philadelphia Centennial Exposition: "Corticelli Conquers," declared *The New York Times* on October 28, 1876. Corticelli's advertising mascot was a kitten playing with a ball of silk that did not tangle, and that image was one of the first large electric billboards in Times Square (see Figures 228 and 229).

As with other thread companies, Nonotuck issued manuals of embroidery that also served as advertisements (see Figure 230). The first was issued in 1887, and Candace Wheeler submitted designs. A rather lovely conventionalized brown lotus or water lily design by Corticelli is shown in Figure 231. It's a long linen runner embroidered in silk.

Figure 228. Front of postcard featuring Corticelli neon kitten, Times Square, New York.

Figure 229. Reverse of Corticelli postcard.

Figure 230. *Corticelli Home Needlework* catalog.

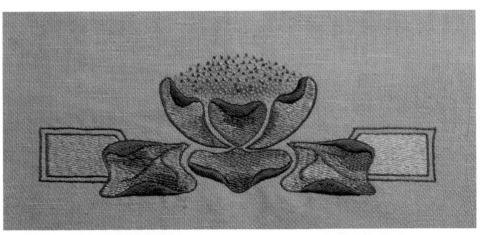

Figure 231. Linen runner, embroidered in silk, water lily design by Corticelli. *Collection of L. Teresa Di Biase.*

Royal Society

One of the most successful makers of patterns, kits, and silks was Royal Society. Rather than some kind of British institution (and not the Royal School of Art Needlework), Royal Society was a brand name of the H.E. Verran company of New York.

Harry E. Verran (1869–1930) was born in Platteville, Wisconsin. He moved to New York around 1900 and went to work at the Bentley Brothers factory on lower Broadway. Bentley Brothers was a New York company established in 1859 that was offering "novelties in art needlework and embroidery" by 1881. In 1886, Charles E. Bentley, the company president, used the trademark Royal Society to sell floss and thread. He registered the trademark in 1909. Verran, who by then had worked his way up to director of Bentley Brothers, purchased the rights to the Royal Society name (and possibly the mill on Union Square) on December 12, 1912. (Bentley continued to sell art needlework kits under the name Artamo.)

The new H.E. Verran Company, Art Needlework, then began selling the extremely popular designs we love today. Verran sold stamped fabric, or iron-on transfers, or entire kits. Each kit included the stamped fabric, floss, and even a needle. The kits were much cheaper than some others (probably why so many finished articles still exist today) because Royal Society kits used either cotton floss or Celesta "art silk" (rayon).

Figures 232, 233, and 234 show variants of the American Beauty design, which dates from 1911. This is clearly derived from the Glasgow Style. (Compare this with Figure 235, a design done by a Glaswegian lady, Miss Runciemann, in 1910.) Pattern numbers in this style range from 590-600.

Figure 232. Royal Society *American Beauty* runner. *Photo by Simone Chaves Kullberg.*

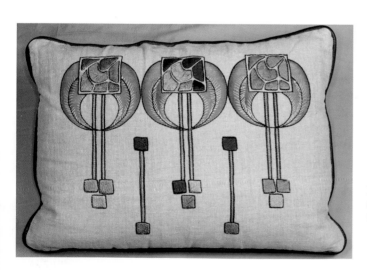

Figure 233. Royal Society *American Beauty* cushion, embroidered and stenciled, leather backing added later. *Collection of Jessica Greenway.*

Figure 234. Royal Society *American Beauty* bag, stenciled and embroidered. *Collection of Kim Covey.*

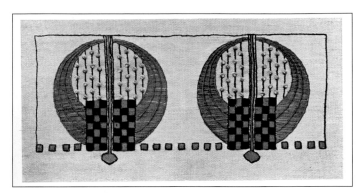

Figure 235. Embroidery design by Glasgow worker Miss Runciemann, *The Studio Volume 50.*

Figures 236, 237, and 238 show a sunflower design from 1919, a kind of Prairie-School-Meets-Vienna-Secession look.

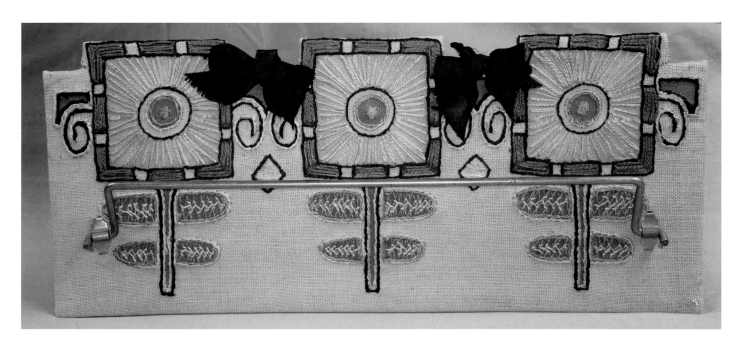

Figure 236. Royal Society sunflower design wall rack. *Collection of Kim Covey.*

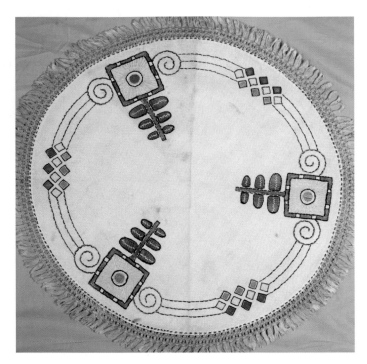

Figure 237. Royal Society sunflower design table center. *Collection of Kim Covey.*

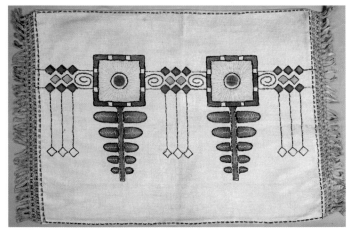

Figure 238. Royal Society sunflower design cushion. *Collection of Kim Covey.*

Royal Society pattern number 177 is shown in Figure 239. The linen was stamped with the color before embroidering. The pine cone pillow in Figure 240 is Royal Society pattern #5187.

Figure 239. Stenciled and embroidered table center by Royal Society. *Collection of Jane Roe.*

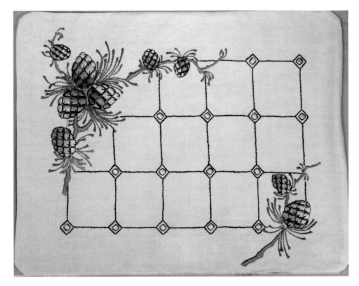

Figure 240. Linen pine cone pillow by Royal Society. *Collection of Lorrie Moore.*

Figure 241 shows a brochure advertising Royal Society package outfits and a Glasgow Style bag made from one shown in the brochure. Figure 242 is the cover of a Royal Society catalog of needlework designs. Notice the cotton on the front—there was a bitter rivalry between makers of cotton thread and makers of silk.

Three items whose makers I am not entirely certain about, but which are certainly in the style of Royal Society, are Figures 243 to 245.

In the late 1920s, Verran built a new factory in Stamford, Connecticut, and moved the company there. He changed the name of the company to Royal Society. At his death in 1930, the firm was sold, though the Royal Society brand name lived on.

Figure 241. Round stenciled and embroidered Glasgow rose bag by Royal Society and package outfit catalog. Design number 316 was fifty cents.

Figure 243. Bag in the style of Royal Society, embroidered and stenciled. *Collection of Lorrie Moore.*

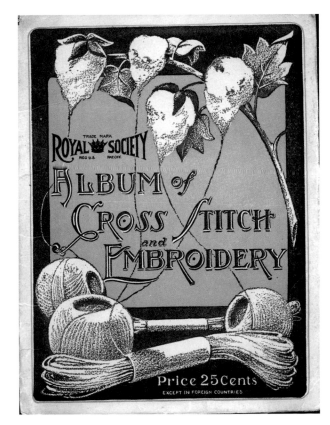

Figure 242. *Royal Society Album of Cross-stitch and Embroidery*, c. 1914.

Figure 244. Embroidered and stenciled runner. *Collection of Kim Covey.*

Figure 245. Embroidered linen runner. *Collection of Kim Covey.*

113

Artamo was a brand name for art needlework patterns made by the Bentley-Franklin Company, which patented the name Artamo in 1911 after it sold its Royal Society name to Verran. (Bentley Brothers later changed its name to Bentley-Franklin.)

After World War I, G. Reis & Bro., a German-owned label company, bought the rights to the Artamo name (see Figure 246). (During the war, G. Reis was managed by a United States Alien Property Custodian, as it was enemy-owned.)

Reis-made Artamo package outfits included DMC cotton. They did not manufacture the thread themselves. Artamo seems to have continued as a brand well into the 1920s, offering kits for children's and ladies' clothing as well as cushions and table covers (see Figures 247 and 248).

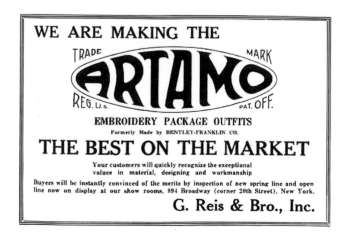

Figure 246. Artamo advertisement.

Figure 247. Peacock table center by Artamo. *Collection of Kim Covey.*

Figure 248. Owl table center by Artamo. *Collection of Jessica Greenway.*

Brainerd & Armstrong

The Brainerd & Armstrong Company of New London, Connecticut, produced wash silks, embroidery silks, silks for knitting, and lining fabric. Originally their goods were manufactured by Nonotuck, but then they built their own factories. James P. Brainerd and Benjamin A. Armstrong formed their company in 1867, after working as silk merchants in New York City. (It was also on Lower Broadway, where Verran had worked.)

Brainerd & Armstrong built its factory in New London, Connecticut, in 1879 (see Figure 249). Brainerd & Armstrong manufactured silk thread and was also well known for their needlework books, particularly their *Embroidery Lessons* series of books featuring colorful illustrations (see Figure 250).

As with many of the needlework companies, patterns were in art needlework style in the 1880s and 1890s, started to resemble art nouveau from about 1900–1910, and started to add Arts and Crafts designs around 1910. Of course, many patterns were continued for many years, so even in 1910, the majority of designs resembled what we would have called art needlework now, with shaded, dimensional designs. Figures 251 to 254 show some interesting designs from various editions of *Embroidery Lessons*.

Figure 249. Brainerd & Armstrong factory postcard.

Figure 251. Page from Brainerd & Armstrong *Embroidery Lessons*.

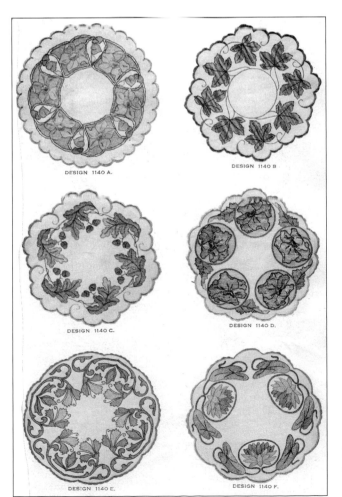

Figure 250. Page from Brainerd & Armstrong *Embroidery Lessons*.

DESIGN 3013 A.

DESIGN 3013 B.

DESIGN 3014.

DESIGN 3015.

DESIGN 3013 C.

DESIGN 3013 D.

PLATE 155.   SOFA   CUSHIONS.
BRAINERD & ARMSTRONG'S WASH EMBROIDERY SILKS.

Figure 252. Page from Brainerd & Armstrong
Embroidery Lessons.

CUSHION No. 3007.

SCARF No. 2007.

CUSHION No. 3012.

SCARF No. 2012.

CUSHION No. 3006.

SCARF No. 2006.

PLATE 154.   SOFA CUSHIONS AND SCARFS.
BRAINERD & ARMSTRONG'S WASH EMBROIDERY SILKS.

Figure 253. Page from Brainerd & Armstrong
Embroidery Lessons.

Figure 254. Page from Brainerd &
Armstrong *Embroidery Lessons.*

Because silk was much more expensive than cotton or rayon, silk companies like Brainerd put out educational booklets insisting that silk was best for embroidery. The year 1909 saw the publication of *Silk: The Real versus the Imitation*, which reminds us that Good Silk is the First Requisite of Good Work. "Page 33 of this book, in mentioning imitation and sham silk, refers to the process by which cotton and linen threads are 'mercerized' and, to an extent, given the appearance of being silk threads. Embroiderers should not for a minute think that these threads are the equal or will give the satisfactory results of a silk embroidery thread. Cotton and linen threads are vegetable fiber, and silk thread is an animal fiber. A thread of animal fiber will take dye better and hold its color faster and longer than a thread of vegetable fiber. The silk thread does not split and fray with age."

Figures 255 and 256 show two conventionalized flower design pillows from Brainerd & Armstrong. Figure 257 is a stenciled table round, unfinished, with the spare thread tacked in a corner. This was known as the conventionalized cornucopia in the catalog.

Figure 255. Linen pillow by Brainerd & Armstrong. *Photo by Simone Chaves Kullberg.*

Figure 256. Embroidered linen pillow by Brainerd & Armstrong, modern leather back. *Collection of Jessica Greenway.*

Figure 257. *Conventionalized Cornucopia* stenciled and embroidered table round, by Brainerd & Armstrong. *Collection of Kim Covey.*

Figure 258 shows a page from *Home Needlecraft* magazine, August 1910, with a design of a pond lily shown in Figure 254 from Brainerd & Armstrong. The article says, "The arts and crafts designs will keep their popularity, but the severity of the conventional lines is being slightly softened by the introduction of the floral patterns."

Brainerd & Armstrong merged with Nonotuck in 1922 (see below).

Figure 258. *Home Needlecraft* magazine, August 1910, design for pond lily.

Heminway

Gen. Merritt Heminway was born in East Haven, Connecticut, in 1800. By 1821, he was established as a merchant in Watertown, Connecticut. In 1849, he began the manufacture of "sewing silks of all kinds." In 1876, Linus Pierpont Brockett wrote a book published by the Silk Association of America called *The Silk Industry in America: A History, Prepared for the Centennial Exposition.* He noted, "If question should ever be debated as to who was the first to introduce spool silks to take the place of skeins in the market [OK then!], Mr. Heminway can advance strong claims to that honor. His manufacture of sewing-silk and twist bears high repute, because of its uniform excellence. As the business increased, his four sons and only daughter obtained an interest in it, and it is still continued, under the firm name of M. Heminway & Sons Silk Co., at the same place."

And of course, like other silk manufacturing companies, M. Heminway produced a number of art embroidery pamphlets. Figure 259 shows a design of grapes from *A Treatise on Art Needlework with Twenty Color Plates*, c. 1910.

After the war, Heminway consolidated with Hammond, Knowlton and Co., a silk manufacturer in operation prior to 1892, to form the HKH Silk Company. In early 1925, the company changed its name to the Heminway Silk Corporation to reflect its major brand name.

Figure 259. Embroidered grape design from *A Treatise on Art Needlework with Twenty Color Plates*, c. 1910.

Belding

Belding, Michigan, is known as the Silk City. It was named after the Belding family who owned four silk mills there. Belding Brothers also had mills in Rockville, Connecticut; Northampton, Massachusetts; Petaluma, California; and Montreal, Canada. Belding was a very large company for its day. The Belding brothers—Milo M., Hiram H., Alvah N., and David W.—also controlled Belding Building Loan Association, Belding Land Improvement Company, Hotel Belding, and Citizens Electric Light Company.

In 1860, Hiram and Alvah started selling silk door to door from their home in Michigan. The family originally came from Massachusetts, the home of much silk production. Milo still lived in Ashfield, Massachusetts, and sent them the silk to sell. This enterprise was very successful. In 1866, the Belding brothers began manufacturing silk thread in Rockville, Connecticut, and in 1872 they expanded to an additional mill in Northampton, Massachusetts, where they manufactured embroidery silks. By 1909, they had built four mills in Belding, Michigan: one for silk thread, two for fabrics, and one for sewing and embroidery silks as well as cotton for crochet. The first mill they built in Michigan was in 1886; it was immediately sold to the Richardson Silk Company because the Beldings wanted to make sure it would be successful before they put their name on it. They bought it back in 1907. The building is still standing but it is an apartment block now.

By 1920, Belding was the largest producer of silk in the United States. With regard to art embroidery, it only sold silk thread—not cotton or "art silk." This meant that its kits tended to be more expensive than its competitors'.

The company produced a catalog and instruction guide called *Needle & Hook* every year (see Figure 260).

Richardson Silk Company

The Richardson Silk Company was formed in 1887 to utilize the first mill in Belding, Michigan, built by the Belding company. George P. Richardson was the founder. By 1915 the company had branched out into cotton threads as well to capture the crochet market. Figure 261 shows a conventionalized lotus design pillow made by the company, which was headquartered in Chicago.

Richardson advertised heavily in the newspapers and also put out embroidery guides (see Figures 262 and 263). One interesting marketing plan they had included the Richardson Art Embroidery Clubs, The Largest Organization Of Its Kind In The World, which entitled you to free instructions in the art of embroidery. Sadly, I have been unable to locate any of the club booklets.

I have been able to find meeting notices in old newspapers, though. For example, the *Beaver* [Oklahoma] *Herald*, April 15, 1909, notes that "The Richardson Art Embroidery Club were pleasantly entertained at the home of Mrs. G. H. Healy, Friday afternoon. Luncheon was served. Misses Edna Beardsley, Bessie Sims, Mae Maple, Albina Hallock, and Alta Roach enjoyed the hospitality of the Club on this occasion, as guests." I bet they had chicken salad.

Figure 261. Lotus pillow, Richardson's pattern #7014, Russian crash (linen) fabric. *Collection of Lorrie Moore.*

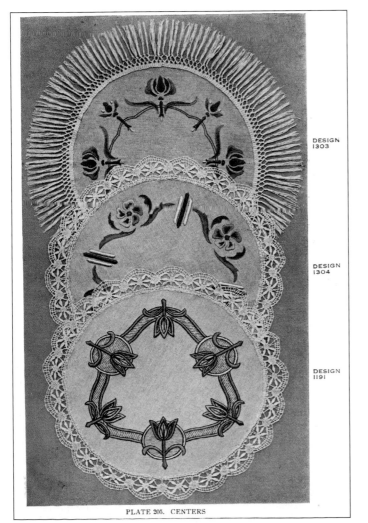

DESIGN 1303

DESIGN 1304

DESIGN 1191

PLATE 205. CENTERS

Figure 260. Embroidery designs from Belding's *Needle & Hook.*

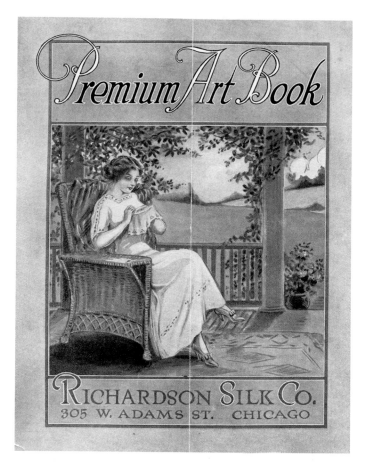

Figure 262. Richardson's *Premium Art Book*, c. 1912.

The Carlson Currier Company of Petaluma, California, was the only silk thread factory west of Michigan. It started as a San Francisco branch of Belding in 1876, but by 1880 it was incorporated. Figure 264 shows a pillow by Carlson Currier with a pattern of Concord grapes.

After an economic slump in 1920, the silk trade declined. "Art silk" (rayon) was much cheaper to manufacture, and mercerized cotton was increasingly used in manufacturing instead of silk thread. Belding Brothers & Company merged with Heminway Silk Company in 1925 and did business as Belding-Heminway. In 1922, the Nonotuck Silk Company merged with the Brainerd & Armstrong Company to form the Corticelli Silk Company. The Corticelli Silk Company then merged in 1932 with the Belding-Heminway Company. Belding-Heminway still exists as a maker of thread as a division of a larger company in Quebec.

Figure 264. Carlson Currier "C. Grape" pattern #169 design pillow. *Collection of Jessica Greenway.*

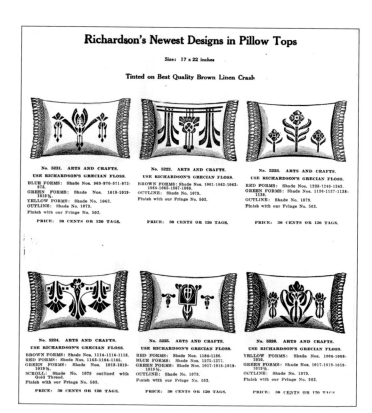

Figure 263. "Arts and Crafts" design pillow tops from Richardson's *Premium Art Book.*

Unknown Makers and Designers

Of course, most Arts and Crafts embroidery today can't be attributed to specific makers. Popular motifs included butterflies and dragonflies (see Figures 265 to 274), which were also very popular in European Arts and Crafts designs and art nouveau.

Figure 267. Embroidered, linen-covered cardboard butterfly wall pocket. *Collection of Kim Covey.*

Figure 265. Design from *Home Needlecraft* magazine, October 1918.

Figure 266. Embroidered butterfly hanging rack. *Collection of Kim Covey.*

Figure 268. Embroidered and stenciled butterfly design. *Collection of Kim Covey.*

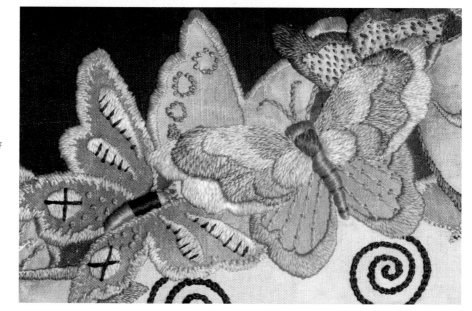

Figure 270. Close up of embroidered cushion with butterflies. *Collection of Lorrie Moore.*

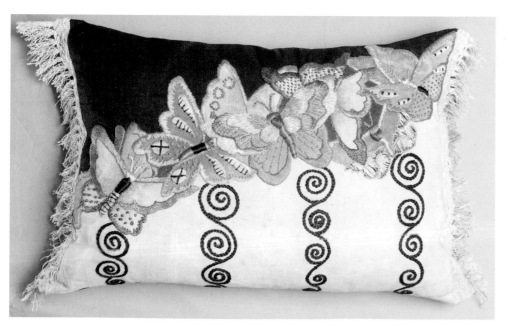

Figure 269. Embroidered, stenciled cushion with butterflies. *Collection of Lorrie Moore.*

Figure 271. Dragonfly tea cozy, labeled inside "Jenny Rae." Possibly Scottish. *Collection of Lorrie Moore.*

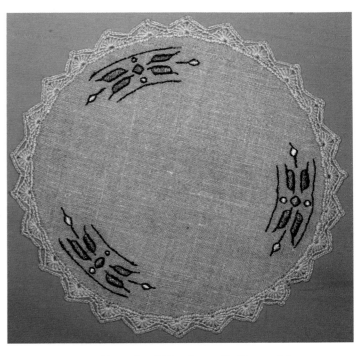

Figure 272. Heavily stylized blue butterfly linen table center. *Collection of Lorrie Moore.*

Figure 273. Linen butterfly doily. *Collection of Lorrie Moore.*

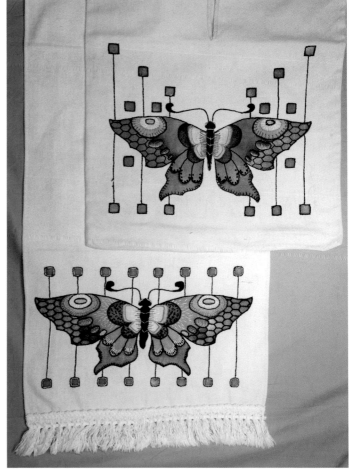

Figure 274. Stenciled and embroidered butterfly runner and bag. These are separate items and were purchased at different times. *Collection of Jessica Greenway.*

Flowers are of course perennially popular as a design. Some flower designs lend themselves easily to conventionalization, so were extremely popular. These include roses, of course (see Figures 275 to 281), and poppies (see Figures 282 to 287). Other examples shown include wisteria, snapdragon, California poppy, nasturtiums, iris, marigold, honeysuckle, trumpet vine, bachelor button, holly, chrysanthemum, and violets—very comprehensive (Figures 288 to 299). The lady slipper design in Figure 300 was featured in *Home Needlework* magazine, December 1911. Of course, some flower designs are just abstract, not meant to be realistic (see Figures 301 to 317). Figure 313 shows more Wallachian work.

Figure 276. Embroidered linen. *Collection of Kim Covey.*

Figure 275. Embroidered linen table topper, handmade lace edging. *Collection of Kim Covey.*

Figure 277. Embroidered linen doily, lace edge. *Collection of Kim Covey.*

Figure 278. Embroidered linen table topper, crocheted lace edging. *Collection of Jessica Greenway.*

Figure 279. Embroidered linen, fagoted edge. *Collection of Jane Roe.*

Figure 280. Linen table runner. *Collection of L. Teresa Di Biase.*

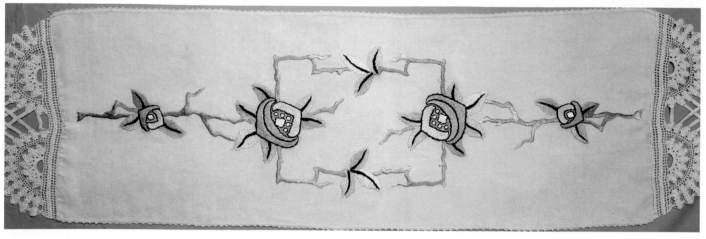

Figure 281. Embroidered linen runner. *Collection of Lorrie Moore.*

Figure 282. Embroidered poppies cushion.
Collection of Faire Ferrill Lees.

Figure 283. Poppy runner.
Collection of Jessica Greenway.

Figure 284. Applied poppy flower round with handmade bobbin lace edging. *Collection of Jessica Greenway.*

Figure 285. Luncheon cloth with fringed edge and ivy leaves. *Collection of Lorrie Moore.*

Figure 286. Embroidered and stenciled pillow cover. *Collection of Lorrie Moore.*

Figure 287. Yellow poppy round edged with tape.
Collection of Faire Ferrill Lees.

Figure 288. Wisteria embroidered cushion.
Collection of Faire Ferrill Lees.

Figure 289. Snapdragon embroidered table cover.
Collection of Faire Ferrill Lees.

Figure 290. California poppy embroidered round. *Collection of Faire Ferrill Lees.*

Figure 291. Nasturtium embroidered luncheon set. *Collection of Kim Covey.*

Figure 292. Stenciled and embroidered iris design cushion cover. *Collection of Jessica Greenway.*

Figure 293. Flower (marigold?) design table cover. Notice the thread color change halfway, where the embroiderer ran out. *Collection of Jessica Greenway.*

Figure 294. Honeysuckle pattern embroidered table cover. *Collection of Jane Roe.*

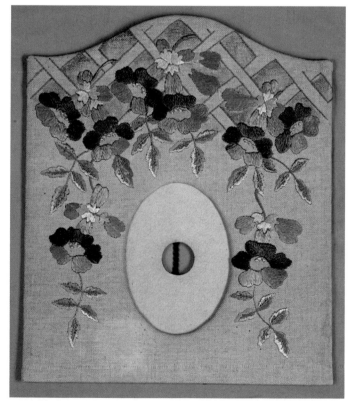

Figure 295. Stenciled and embroidered linen picture frame. *Collection of Kim Covey.*

Figure 296. Embroidered blue flowered round.
Collection of Jane Roe.

Figure 297. Embroidered linen round with holly.
Collection of Faire Ferrill Lees.

Figure 298. Stylized chrysanthemum pattern linen cushion. *Collection of Jessica Greenway.*

Figure 299. Stenciled and embroidered violet cushion, modern leather back. *Collection of Jessica Greenway.*

Figure 300. Stylized ladyslipper pattern linen table cover. *Collection of Jane Roe.*

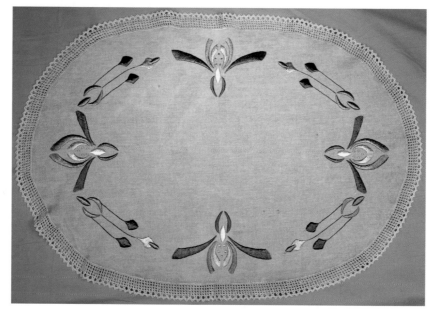

Figure 301. Stylized flower linen table cover with crochet edge. *Collection of Jessica Greenway.*

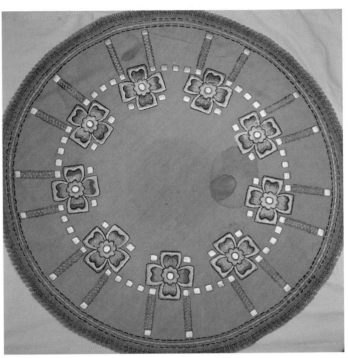

Figure 302. Embroidered blue flower bedcover. *Collection of Kim Covey.*

Figure 303. Stylized flower orange linen round. *Collection of Kim Covey.*

Figure 304. Embroidered blue flower linen reticule—bone rings. *Collection of Kim Covey.*

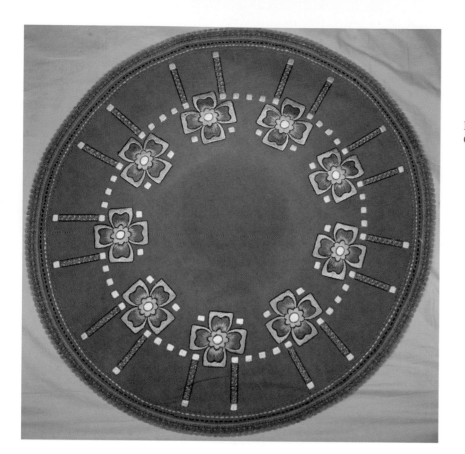

Figure 305. Stylized flower brown linen round. *Collection of Kim Covey.*

Figure 306. Brown and beige embroidered linen cushion cover. *Collection of L. Teresa Di Biase.*

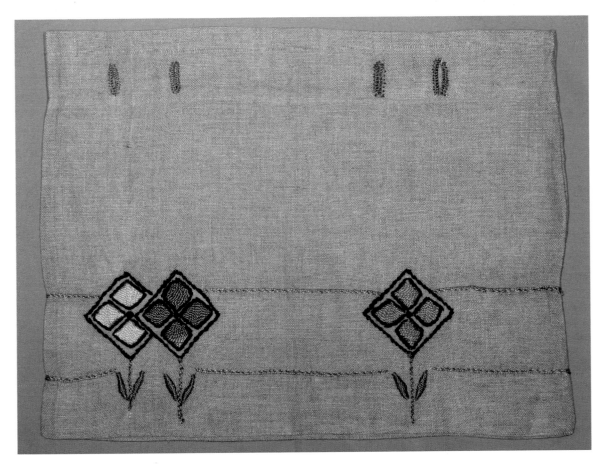

Figure 307. Very stylized flower linen reticule. *Collection of Lorrie Moore.*

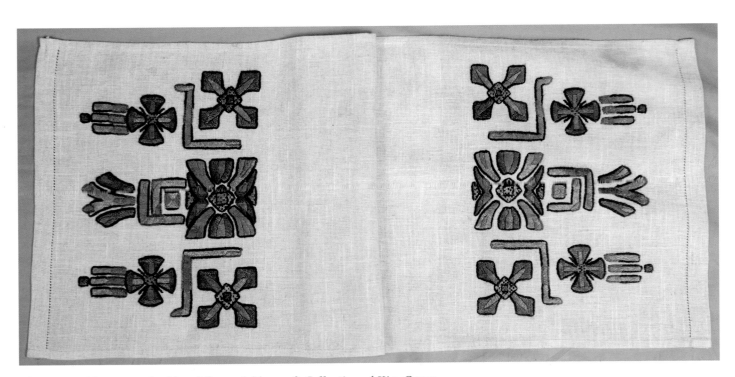

Figure 308. Abstract embroidered flower table scarf. *Collection of Kim Covey.*

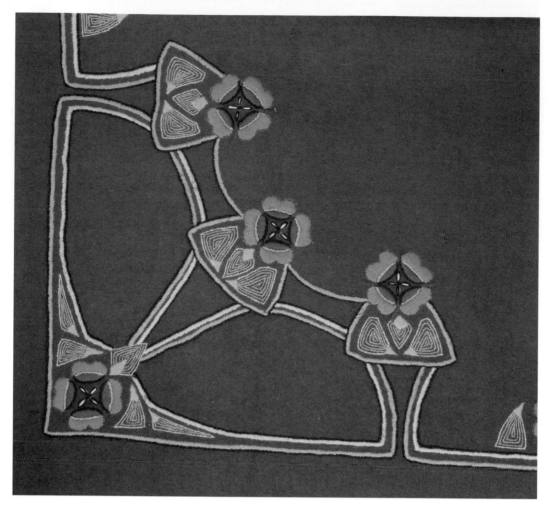

Figure 309. Green wool table cover, crewel stitching. *Collection of Kim Covey.*

Figure 310. Pale green abstract flowers. *Collection of Jane Roe.*

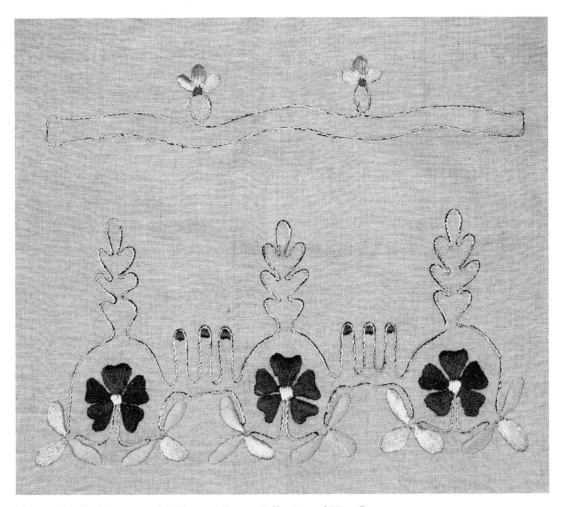

Figure 311. Red flower embroidery on linen. *Collection of Kim Covey.*

Figure 312. Abstract embroidered flower table round. *Collection of Kim Covey.*

Figure 313. Wallachian stitch table round. *Collection of Jane Roe.*

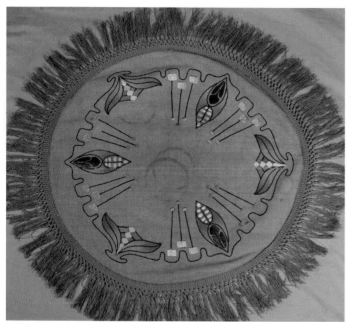

Figure 314. Abstract embroidered flower table round with fringed edge. *Collection of Kim Covey.*

Figure 315. Floral embroidered linen oval. *Collection of Kim Covey.*

Figure 316. Abstract embroidered table round. *Collection of Kim Covey.*

Figure 317. Table mat, linen with a colorful embroidered design. *Courtesy Treadway Gallery.*

Some designs showed the influence of art nouveau from Europe (see Figures 318 through 325). Figure 325 is a whiplash design center very similar to ideas coming out of France and Germany. Poppies (see Figure 320) seem to have been much more popular in America than in Europe, though the squares on this design are directly from Glasgow and Vienna. Figure 321 isn't art nouveau, but the galleon design was very popular in the British Arts and Crafts movement and almost unknown in the U.S.

Figure 319. Nouveau red flower frame, cardboard backed. *Collection of Kim Covey.*

Figure 318. Art nouveau style chrysanthemum oblong. *Collection of Kim Covey.*

Figure 320. Vienna or Glasgow influenced poppy frame.
Collection of Kim Covey.

Figure 321. Appliquéd and embroidered galleon design, possibly British. *Collection of Lorrie Moore.*

Figure 322. Stylized design linen bag.
Collection of Kim Covey.

Figure 323. Glove or jewelry box with embroidered flowers. *Collection of Kim Covey.*

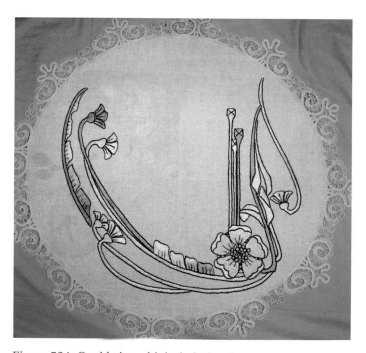

Figure 324. Oval beige whiplash design flowers. *Collection of Jane Roe.*

Figure 325. Embroidered tulip linen book cover. *Collection of Kim Covey.*

Pinecones were popular (see Figure 326), as were Native American designs (these owe nothing to Europe), as shown in Figures 327 and 328. Scarabs and Egyptian motifs become popular in the later days of Arts and Crafts as tombs were uncovered by archaeologists (see Figures 329 to 332). The two bags are almost certainly by Royal Society.

Figure 326. Stenciled and embroidered pinecone design round, couched needles. *Collection of Lorrie Moore.*

Figure 327. Stylized design embroidered linen cushion cover. *Collection of Jessica Greenway.*

Figure 329. Cushion cover, colorful dyed, and embroidered Egyptian motif. *Courtesy Treadway Gallery.*

Figure 328. Native American design stenciled and appliquéd bag with wicker bottom. *Collection of Lorrie Moore.*

Figure 330. Stylized design embroidered linen table round. *Collection of Kim Covey.*

Figure 331. Stenciled and embroidered scarab design bag. Brass tab front with original green ribbon looped through metal clasp. Probably Royal Society. *Collection of Lorrie Moore.*

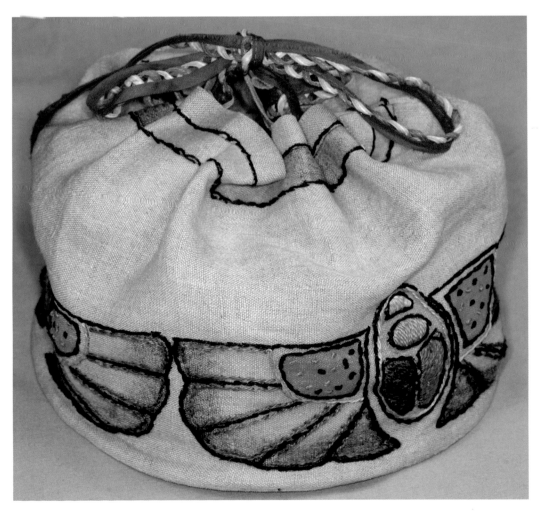

Figure 332. Stenciled and embroidered scarab design bag, leather braided handle. Probably Royal Society. *Collection of Kim Covey.*

Grapes were also a popular American design (see Figures 333 to 336). I like how the pillow in Figure 333 shows white grapes as well as purple—that's unusual. Figure 337 has me confused—it looks like a grapevine, but with an artichoke or a pinecone on it. Oh well, it's charming, which is the main thing.

Figure 333. Grape embroidered pillow with modern leather back. *Collection of Jessica Greenway.*

Figure 334. Table round with stenciled and embroidered grapevine. *Courtesy Treadway Gallery.*

Figure 335. Silk table square with embroidered orange grapes. *Collection of Kim Covey.*

Figure 336. Stenciled and embroidered grapes cloth. *Collection of Faire Ferrill Lees.*

Figure 337. Mystery vegetation with crochet lace edging. *Collection of Lorrie Moore.*

Finally, we get to Figure 338—very possibly my favorite American design in this book. "Smoke and Cast Away All Care." Please note the burn marks on the piece, evidence that the lady took the pillow's advice. In fact, she was apparently so carefree she couldn't even be bothered to finish the piece. Rock on, 1910s lady.

Figure 338. Linen embroidered cushion cover, by the lady who liked to smoke. *Collection of Kim Covey.*

Chapter 9
Dress

Arts and Crafts embroidery wasn't only used on household items—women and children wore it on dresses, smocks, aprons, and undergarments. Of course, clothing has always been adorned with embroidery, but the artistic dress adopted by the Aesthetic Movement made one's personal style a reflection of one's artistic principles.

Fashionable Victorian ladies' clothing was ridiculous. It was hot, impractical, uncomfortable, prevented the wearer from taking enough exercise, and was health-endangering. Tight-laced corsets deformed the figure and squeezed the internal organs.

In the middle to late nineteenth century, there were several different movements to reform women's dress. For our purposes, the first important one was the artistic dress movement which started in the 1860s with the Pre-Raphaelite artists. These artists rejected the current fashion of corsets and crinolines and garbed their models in soft, trailing dresses based on adapted fashions of the past, such as Regency or Empire dresses, romanticized medieval gowns, or classical Grecian modes. Artistic dresses were loose

and uncorseted and were made in vegetable-dyed fabrics with soft colors, not the harsh, bright aniline dyes, and were ornamented with embroidery. The effect was sensuous and languid.

These fashions eventually were reflected in the Aesthetic Movement of the 1870s and 1880s. Aesthetic ladies wore simple dresses without bustles, corsets, or trains. Embroidery on your dresses showed that you had leisure time and artistic taste. The dresses often had sunflowers, lilies, daffodils or daisies embroidered on them, symbols of the movement. Colors were the soft, "greenery-yallery" colors, possibly an exotic peacock blue as well. The hero of the movement, Oscar Wilde, proclaimed "One should either be a work of art or wear a work of art."

Punch enjoyed mocking the pretensions of the Aesthetes; Figure 339 shows a cartoon of a fashionable lady as seen by an Aesthetic lady and an Aesthetic lady as seen by a fashionable lady. Despite the mockery, many of the decorative features of Aesthetic dress showed up in mainstream 1890s fashion.

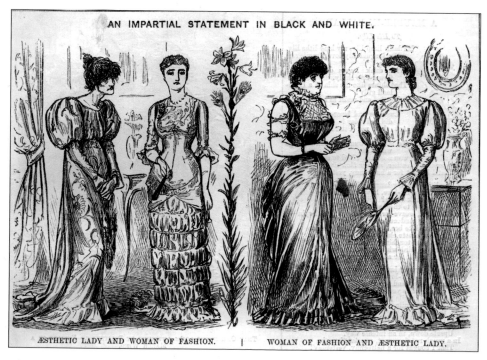

Figure 339. Cartoon from *Punch*, April 9, 1881.

Loosely cut, simple dresses needed embroidery for decoration. Embroidery associated clothing with handwork rather than machine work, so it was more artistic; it was also relatively inexpensive as compared to other dress materials used on Victorian clothing such as fur, beads, or lace.

Figure 340 shows a coat, c. 1895, covered with hand embroidery of an English wildflower called sweet cicely. The fabric is purple silk velvet, and the embroidery is yellow and green silk, with petals of white felt. The medieval style collar reflects artistic dress; wildflowers were popular Arts and Crafts motifs, evoking simple rural life before the Industrial Revolution. The coat was sold by Marshall and Snelgrove, an exclusive London department store that featured custom dressmaking as Liberty & Co. did.

Girls as well as adult women wore artistic dress, often inspired by the artwork of Kate Greenaway. Eighteenth century mob caps, oversized straw hats, and empire-waisted muslin dresses projected an air of sweetness and innocence from past times, and they were also much less confining for little girls than velvet gowns with bustles and layers of petticoats. Figure 341 shows a child's coat in blue silk lined with cream printed cotton, c. 1885. I think it's actually for a boy. The collar, cuffs, and box-pleats are hand-embroidered in silk with flowers, fruit, and leaves, outlined with couched gold thread; some of the motifs are also decorated with beads.

Figure 341. Blue silk embroidered child's coat, c. 1890, worked with silk threads with flowers, fruit, and leaves in hand-stitched embroidery, couched gold thread, and beads. *Courtesy V&A Images/Victoria and Albert Museum.*

Figure 340. Purple silk velvet embroidered coat, c. 1895-1900, sold by Marshall & Snelgrove. *Courtesy V&A Images/Victoria and Albert Museum.*

Another dress reform movement was based more on health than aesthetics and reflected the growing influence of feminism. The Rational Dress Society was founded in 1881 in London. "The Rational Dress Society protests against the introduction of any fashion in dress that either deforms the figure, impedes the movements of the body, or in any way tends to injure the health. It protests against the wearing of tightly-fitting corsets; of high-heeled shoes; of heavily-weighted skirts, as rendering healthy exercise almost impossible; and of all tie down cloaks or other garments impeding on the movements of the arms. It protests against crinolines or crinolettes of any kind as ugly and deforming …" Oscar Wilde's wife Constance edited all the editions of the *Rational Dress Society Gazette*, where women were told they should "free their bodies and render them fit companions for their enlarged minds."

Eventually the two movements were combined in the Healthy and Artistic Dress Union, begun in 1890, whose vice president was the indefatigable Walter Crane. It produced numerous pamphlets, including "How to Dress without a Corset," illustrated by Crane. It held the first exhibition of artistic dress (you get the feeling that Crane never met a problem that couldn't be solved by a public exhibition) and published the journal *Aglaia*.

A later group attempting to reform taste and craftsmanship in clothing was the Dress Designers' Exhibition Society. Details are sketchy, but the organization seems to have been formed about 1903, possibly in connection with the Art Workers' Guild. I have found references to exhibitions (helloooo Mr. Crane!) from 1903 every year to 1908, which seems to have been the last one. The shows included modern lace, jewelry, embroidery, hand-woven fabrics, and so on.

The dress in Figure 342 was designed by Walter Crane, worked by Edith Swinhoe, and shown at the second Dress Designers' Exhibition in 1904. *Arts and Crafts Magazine* said that the dress was not strikingly original, but that it was good because "more than a very moderate degree of originality in ladies' dress intended for general wear is a bar, rather than an incentive, to its adoption. There is distinct charm in this plain red grisson dress, with its simple black linen appliqué on white couch with black filoselle, and finished with a black and white cord." *The Studio* wrote that the exhibition "was interesting, because it gave a good idea of the scope there is for ingenuity of design in everyday things, and of the capacities of a number of clever workers who have undertaken the heroic task of improving the popular taste in dress and personal adornment."

Figure 342. Embroidered dress designed by Walter Crane. *Arts and Crafts Magazine, Volume 1.*

Figure 343 is a typical Arts and Crafts linen dress, c. 1905, for a young lady. A number of these dresses in this shape and in similar fabrics have surfaced. Figure 344 shows the embroidered yoke from another version in pink linen, the neckline inserted with ivory cotton embroidered with floss silk flower sprays in pink and green.

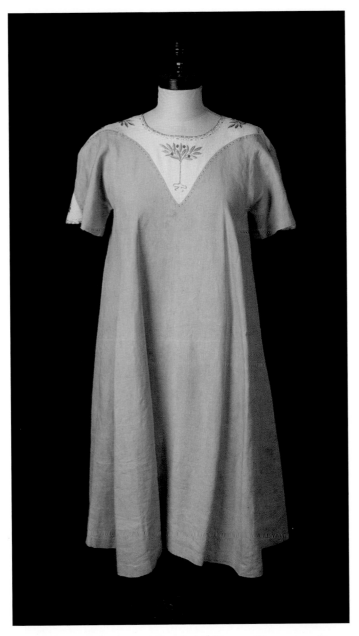

Figure 344. Neckline of pink linen girl's dress embroidered with pinks. *Courtesy Meg Andrews.*

Figure 343. Made circa 1910, of pink linen with a cream linen embroidered yoke, this dress was worn as a child by a Mrs. Spurgin of Abingdon, Oxfordshire. *Photo by Simone Chaves Kullberg.*

Glasgow

Because the Glasgow School of Art had a large percentage of female students, some of the best artistic dress was to be found in Scotland. One lady who liked to dress in her own style was Jessie Newbery (see Figure 345). In the same way William Morris started designing furniture for himself because he couldn't find anything he liked to buy, she designed and often made her own clothes. Beauty and comfort of dress was also important to Mrs. Newbery. She favored an individual style of dress, and often embroidered cuffs, collars, and belts for her own use and for her daughters.

Figure 346. Bodice of silk embroidered and appliquéd maternity dress by Jessie Newbery. *Copyright Manchester Art Gallery.*

Jessie's little girls, Elsie and Mary, wore clothes like hers. (It's interesting how Jessie Newbery's adult dresses and child's dresses are more or less the same.) "The two little Newbery girls were distinctive at parties, and some mothers tried to copy them, but a contemporary remembers that the other children (no doubt echoing the overheard remarks of grown ups) felt sorry for them having to wear clothes designed by their mother. Mary enjoyed wearing them, but feels that Elsie would have liked a dress with a sailor collar and pleated skirt like the others." (*Costume* magazine.) The Newbery girls are shown in their pretty Glasgow Style dresses in Figure 347.

Figure 347 is from a book called *Das Eigenklied der Frau* (*Woman's Individual-Dress*) by Anna Muthesius, wife of the architectural critic Hermann and friend of the Glasgow designers. Mrs. Muthesius promulgated the idea of the "anti-fashion dress" (*Anti-Modekleide*), in which the cut, material, and color of a garment are more important than how closely it hews to the current fashion.

Figure 345. Jessie Newbery, about 1895. *Courtesy Glasgow Museums Photo Library.*

Mrs. Newbery taught the cut and construction of clothing in her embroidery classes, aiming for both beauty and practicality. A dress designed by Jessie Newbery in 1902 is shown in Figure 346. This dress was constructed, as all of Jessie Newbery's were, without a set-in waist. Of white silk, it's actually a nursing/maternity dress. It's open in front and has a concealed fastening below the yoke with buttons. Fullness is cinched in at the waist with a belt that matches the embroidery on the yoke: appliquéd green linen hearts, with green and blue silk embroidery.

Figure 347. Elsie and Mary Newbery in dresses designed by their mother. *Das Eigenkleid der Frau*, Munich: Druck und Verlag 1903.

Another German book, *Moderne Stickereien* (*Modern Embroidery*), published in 1902, printed several Jessie Newbery-designed dresses for little girls, very similar to the actual dresses worn by the Newbery girls (see Figure 348). Two absolutely darling little girls' bonnets from the book are shown in Figure 349. Yes, they're German, but I couldn't resist including them. I can't be the only one wanting to reproduce these hats immediately and shove a modern little girl's head in them.

Figure 348. Girls' dresses designed by Jessie Newbery. *Moderne Stickereien.*

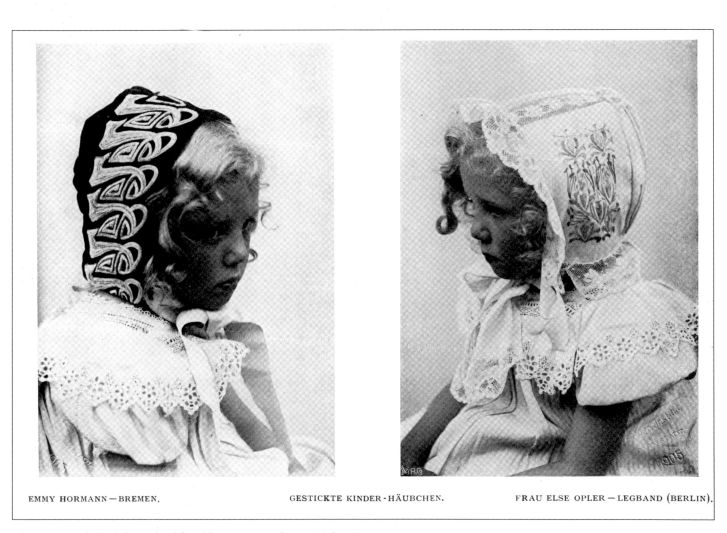

Figure 349. Little girls' embroidered bonnets. *Moderne Stickereien.*

Figure 350 shows Daisy McGlashan and her daughters, Daisy and Agnes Violet, in their adorable Kate Greenaway style dresses and mob caps. Daisy Agnes McGlashan (1879-1968) studied at the Glasgow School of Art from 1889–1905. She designed and embroidered her own clothes and wrote and illustrated children's stories. Both little girls also eventually studied at the Glasgow School of Art and also became artists. (Notice the teddy bears.)

Figure 350. Daisy McGlashan with Daisy and Agnes Violet, c. 1905. *Courtesy of Glasgow School of Art.*

Ann Macbeth, who was known for wearing dresses "covered in embroidery" (see Figure 351), drew some girls' dresses with instructions in her book *Educational Needlecraft*. One is shown in Figure 352. The dress is full, without a set-in waist, only cinched by a yoke.

Figure 351. Ann Macbeth, c. 1900. *Courtesy Glasgow Museums Photo Library.*

Figure 352. Dress designed by Ann Macbeth. *Educational Needlecraft.*

Sometimes entire dresses were embroidered, but
sometimes just parts of dresses or accessories were:
yokes, collars, purses, and so on. Figure 353 shows
a design for an embroidered yoke by Ann Macbeth.
In case you can't figure out how yokes like that
would be worn, Figure 354 shows some embroidered
bodices by Miss Macbeth, as illustrated in *Modern
Practical Design*.

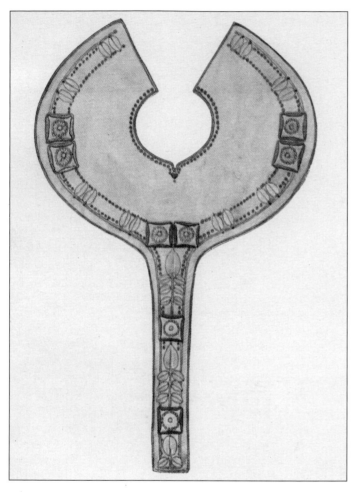

Figure 353. Design for embroidered yoke by Ann Macbeth.
Educational Needlecraft.

Figure 354. Designs for waists by Ann Macbeth.
Modern Practical Design.

Figure 355 shows a collar with a pansy design attributed to Jessie Newbery; Figure 356 shows a collar designed by Ann Macbeth. A later American collar is in Figure 357; what's particularly cool about this collar (besides the fact that it is ivy, a symbol of fidelity) is that the ivy berries are padded and three-dimensional. More American embroidered reticules are shown in Figures 358 and 359; Figure 359 is almost certainly a Royal Society. Figure 360 is a Glasgow Style bag.

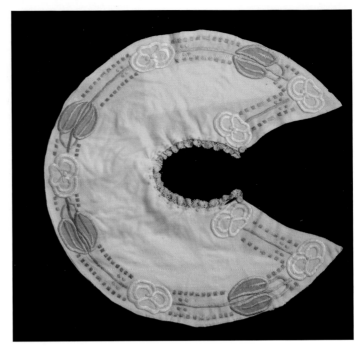

Figure 355. Silk collar with silk embroidered and appliquéd pansies and leaves.

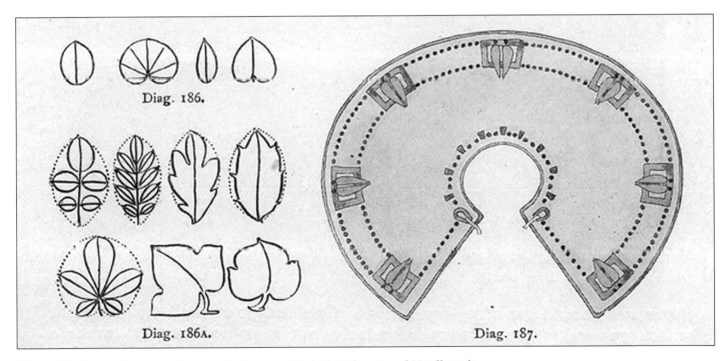

Diag. 186.

Diag. 186A.

Diag. 187.

Figure 356. Design for embroidered collar by Ann Macbeth. *Educational Needlecraft.*

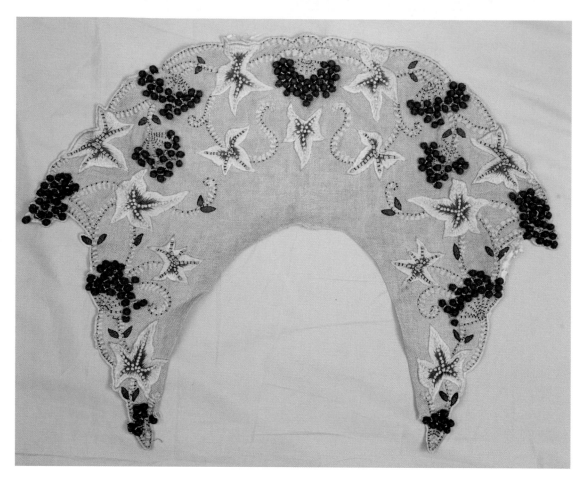

Figure 357. Ivy design collar, padded berries. *Collection of Kim Covey.*

Figure 358. Linen embroidered bag. *Collection of Jessica Greenway.*

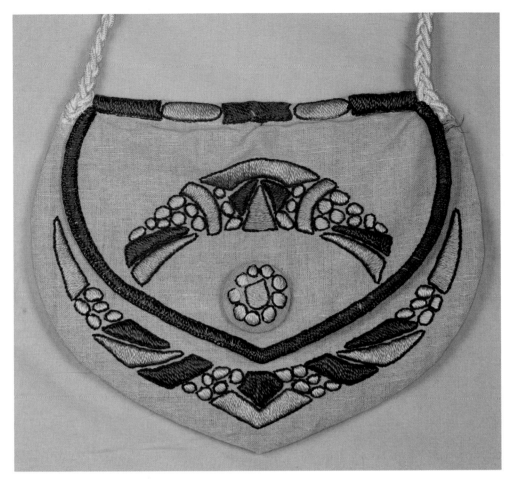

Figure 359. Linen embroidered bag, probably by Royal Society.
Collection of Jessica Greenway.

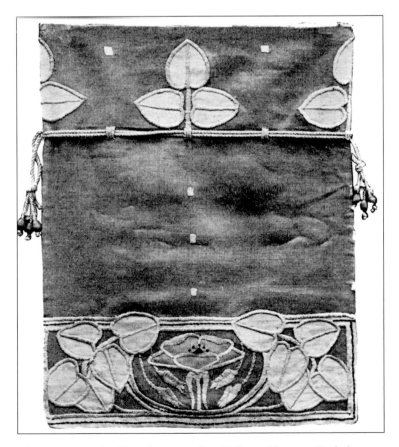

Figure 360. Embroidered and appliquéd linen Glasgow Style bag.
The Studio Volume 53.

Figure 361 shows an incredible embroidered collar trimmed with silver by Rene Lalique (French, but again, couldn't resist). *The Studio* (1905) wrote that this was "the work of an artist possessed of an extraordinary imaginative genius and of a rare and unexampled skill in the use of the most difficult of all materials."

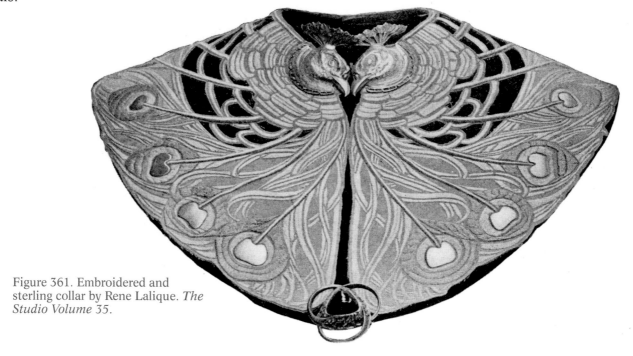

Figure 361. Embroidered and sterling collar by Rene Lalique. *The Studio Volume 35.*

Figure 362 is an extraordinary American reticule with a hammered copper frame, embroidered with peacock feathers. This bag is amazing—the only one I have ever seen with a metal Arts and Crafts frame. It's absolutely beautiful.

Figure 362. Rare American bag with embroidered linen and hammered copper. *Collection of Jane Roe.*

Next is an English collar embroidered in purple and mauve carnations and roses with yellow centers on gold stems and green leaves, all on a natural cotton ground, c. 1905 (see Figure 363).

Embroidered hosiery goes back hundreds of years to medieval times. Today people still like to wear socks with colorful embellishments, but tights (stockings) such as these aren't embroidered, because they are considered disposable. Very few people darn ripped hosiery anymore, so putting hand work into it seems pointless. Figure 364 is a page from a Brainerd & Armstrong catalog of 1912 offering embroidery designs for your stockings, should you get tired of embroidering celery bags.

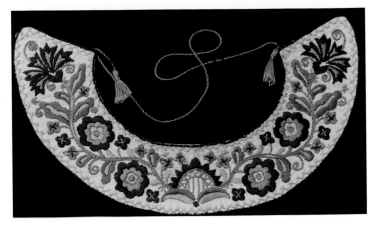

Figure 363. English collar, silk embroidered on cotton.

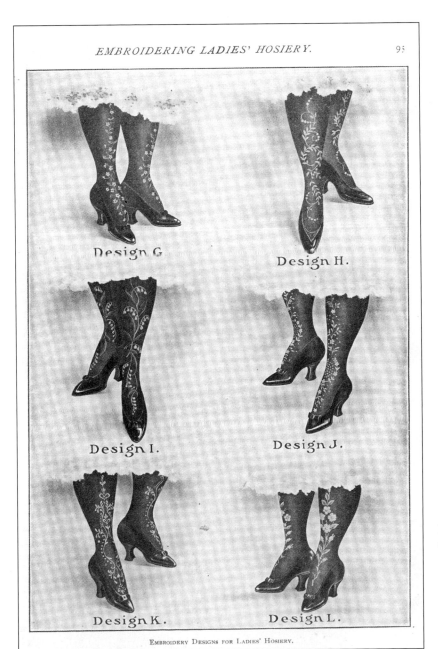

Figure 364. Embroidered stocking designs from c. 1912 Brainerd & Armstrong catalog.

American Clothing

American clothing seems to have lagged behind European when it came to Arts and Crafts decoration. In fact, it never seems to have been very popular; of course, the war probably had something to do with it.

Figure 365 is an illustration of a child's dress stamped for embroidery by Belding. And remember, as we've learned, the first requisite of good work is good silk.

Figure 365. Package outfit for child's dress from Beldings, c. 1910.

Figure 366 shows an ad for patterns for embroidered dresses, including one with a square Glasgow rose design, from the June 1917 issue of *Modern Priscilla* magazine. *Modern Priscilla*, published in Boston, started as a sixteen-page newsletter on 1887 about fancy work, dress patterns, china painting, and needlework in general. It eventually became a women's general interest magazine, but with an emphasis on needlework. It absorbed *Everyday Housekeeping* in March 1912 and *Home Needlework Magazine* in May 1917. The last issue was July 1930, after which it was folded into *Needlecraft*. The Priscilla Needlework Company sold fancy work kits, patterns, and even a privately branded sewing machine, made by the New Home Sewing Machine Company of Massachusetts. The New Home brand name still exists, although the company itself was absorbed by Janome, a Japanese firm, in 1957.

Figure 366. Ad for patterns for embroidered dresses, *Modern Priscilla*, June 1917.

A pretty green linen embroidered Arts and Crafts dress (see Figure 367) with pink trim at the neckline and sleeves and a pointed hem and collar is dated around the same time, c. 1917.

The final dress is late, c. 1924 (see Figure 368). It's a cream linen Arts and Crafts summer dress. The sleeves are embroidered with a brown eyelet pattern and the skirt with vertical bands of the eyelet pattern; a self-fabric belt is also embroidered. The style is reminiscent of the *Wiener Werkstatte*.

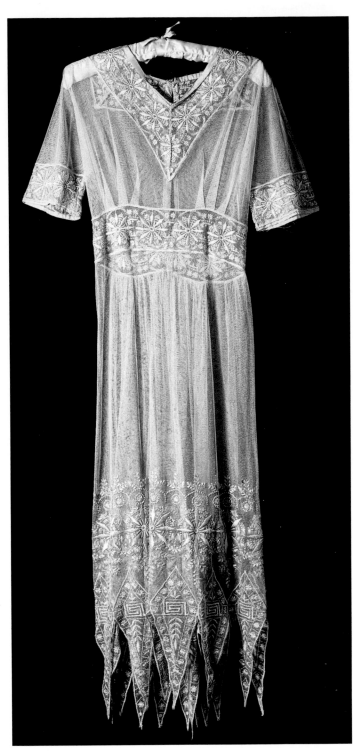

Figure 367. Arts & Crafts dress, green linen with pink trim at the neckline and sleeves, and a pointed hem. *Courtesy Treadway Gallery.*

Figure 368. Cotton summer dress with Viennese-style embroidered eyelet trim, c. 1924. *Copyright Indiana State Museum.*

Chapter 10
Arts and Crafts Embroidery Today

So what happened to Arts and Crafts embroidery? After a long period of unpopularity, it began to be rediscovered in the 1970s and 1980s by the public; well-received Arts and Crafts exhibitions put embroidery on display.

Today, a collector can buy originals, reproduction items, as well as new designs in the Arts and Crafts style. Ann Wallace, at Ann Wallace & Friends Period Textiles in Los Angeles, produces stencil, appliqué, and embroidery designs in the spirit of Gustav Stickley, William Morris, Charles Rennie Mackintosh, and others. The author of *Arts & Crafts Textiles* (Gibbs Smith, 1999), Ann produces hand-embroidered and stenciled table runners, pillows, curtains, and bedding, as well as kits and fabric by the yard (see Figures 369 to 375).

Figure 369. Ginkgo design table round by Ann Wallace. *Courtesy Ann Wallace.*

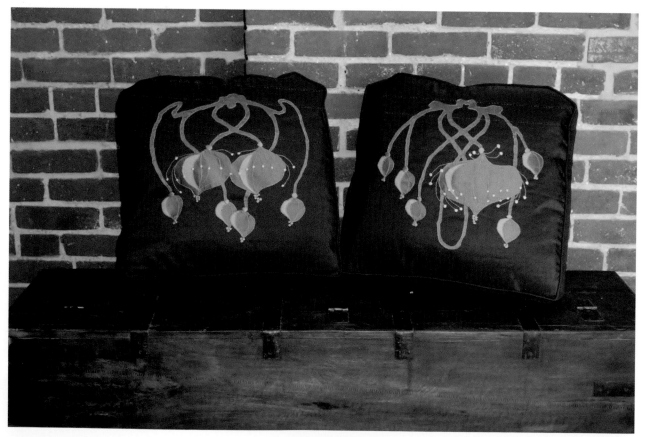

Figure 370. Appliqué cushions by Ann Wallace. *Courtesy Ann Wallace.*

Figure 371. Appliqué cushions by Ann Wallace. *Courtesy Ann Wallace*.

Figure 372. Stenciled napkins by Ann Wallace. *Courtesy Ann Wallace*.

Figure 373. Stenciled and embroidered table runners by Ann Wallace. *Courtesy Ann Wallace*.

Figure 374. Stenciled and embroidered table runners by Ann Wallace. *Courtesy Ann Wallace*.

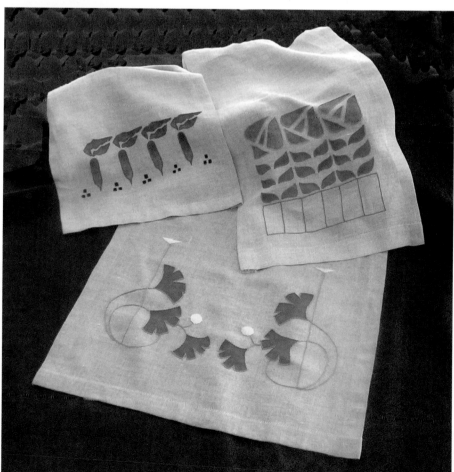

Figure 375. Embroidered bed linen by Ann Wallace. *Courtesy Ann Wallace.*

Figure 376. Embroidered speaker covers by Dianne Ayres.
Courtesy Dianne Ayres.

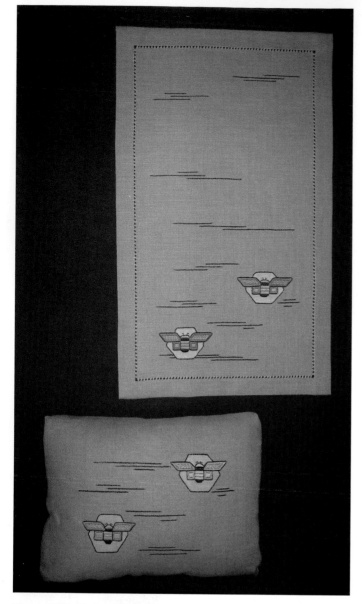

Dianne Ayres, of Arts and Crafts Period Textiles in Oakland, California, believes an Arts and Crafts style home is distinguished as much by its friendly, comfortable atmosphere as it is by its architecture, furniture, and other objects. Coauthor of *American Arts and Crafts Textiles* (Harry N. Abrams, 2002), Dianne creates textiles for the home using turn-of-the-twentieth-century techniques—appliqué, hand embroidery, and hand stenciling. Embroideries are available completed or as kits.

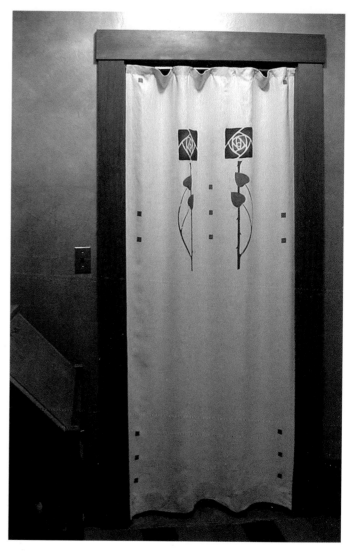

Figure 377. Embroidered bee designs by Dianne Ayres. *Courtesy Dianne Ayres.*

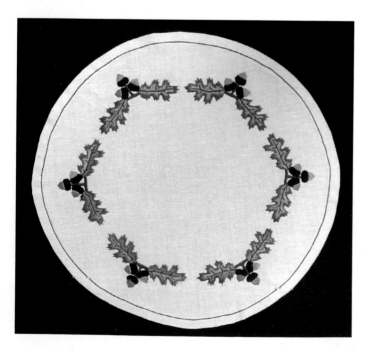

Figure 379. Dard Hunter-style rose portière by Dianne Ayres. *Courtesy Dianne Ayres.*

Figure 378. Embroidered oak design by Dianne Ayres. *Courtesy Dianne Ayres.*

Martha Frankel at Thistle Handwerks in Montana spent twenty years as a historic properties manager, museum curator, and administrator, but yearned for work that was more creative. Her mother and grandmother passed on to her their love of fine fibers and the textile arts; she says her grandmother would stroll through fabric shop aisles with both hands extended, and only stopped when something felt right. In 1995, Martha traveled to Scotland and saw Glasgow Style embroidery; much of her work today is done in this style (see Figures 380 to 382).

Ann Chaves travels around the country to conduct popular embroidery workshops at Arts and Crafts shows. She has been actively working in the Arts and Crafts field for over twenty years; she says her interest in handcrafted textiles was sparked at a young age by her Scottish grandmother who taught her to knit and sew. Her work emphasizes fluid originality rather than mere reproduction of the Arts and Crafts movement. Ann also designs and creates beautiful items on commission at her studio, Inglenook Textiles in Pasadena, California.

David Ford at Ford Craftsman takes a slightly different approach than these ladies. He believes that machine embroidery and "art silk" makes for a high-quality product that looks great, wears well, and is affordable. After all, Gustav Stickley himself believed that machines should be used to do repetitive tasks when they don't reduce the quality and workmanship of the final product. David makes cushions, tote bags, napery, and so on in his shop.

Whether new, old, reproduction, newly designed, handmade, or machine-made, one hundred and fifty years after William Morris began unpicking medieval embroideries, Arts and Crafts embroidery is still well loved.

Figure 380. Appliquéd raven curtains by Martha Frankel. *Photo by Christopher Marona.*

Figure 381. Close up of appliquéd raven curtains by Martha Frankel. *Photo by Christopher Marona.*

Figure 382. Thistle Handwerks collection of the author.

Bibliography

Alford, Marian. *Needlework as Art*. London: Low, 1886.

Arthur, Anne Knox. *An Embroidery Book*. London: A. & C. Black, Ltd., 1920.

Arthur, Liz. *Textile Treasures at the Glasgow School of Art*. London: The Herbert Press, 2005.

Arthur, Liz. *The Unbroken Thread*. Renfrew: Gardner Gibson Print, nd.

Arts and Crafts Essays. London: Rivington, Percival, & Co., 1893.

Arwas, Victor. *Art Nouveau: From Mackintosh to Liberty: the Birth of a Style*. London: Andreas Papadakis Publisher, 2000.

Ayres, Dianne, Timothy Hansen, Beth Ann McPherson, & Tommy Arthur McPherson II. *American Arts and Crafts Textiles*. New York: Harry N. Abrams, 2002.

Bolton, Sarah. "Some Successful Women." *Wide Awake*. Boston: D. Lothrop Company, 1887.

Buck, Anne. *Victorian Costume*. Bedford: Ruth Bean Publishers, 1984.

Burkhauser, Jude (ed.). *Glasgow Girls: Women in Art and Design 1880–1920*. Edinburgh: Canongate Publishing Ltd., 1990.

Callen, Anthea. *Women in The Arts And Crafts Movement, 1870–1914*. London: Astragal Books, 1979.

Calloway, Stephen. *Liberty of London: Masters of Style & Decoration*. London: Thames and Hudson Ltd., 1992.

Carruthers, Annette & Mary Greensted, ed. *Simplicity or Splendor*. Cheltenham: Cheltenham Art Gallery and Museums, 1999.

Christie, Mrs. Archibald H. [Grace]. *Samplers and Stitches*. London: B.T. Batsford, 1920.

Cluckie, Linda. *The Rise and Fall of Art Needlework*. Bury St. Edmonds: Arena Books, 2008.

Cooper, Jeremy. *Victorian and Edwardian Décor: From the Gothic Revival to Art Nouveau*. New York: Abbeville Press, 1987.

Crane, Walter. *Ideals in Art*. London: George Bell and Sons, 1905.

Crouch, Christopher. *Design Culture in Liverpool 1880–1914*. Liverpool: Liverpool University Press, 2002.

Cumming, Elizabeth. *Hand, Heart and Soul: The Arts and Crafts Movement in Scotland*. Edinburgh: Birlinn Limited, 2006.

Day, Lewis F. *The Magazine of Fine Arts*. London: G. Newnes, 1905.

Day, Lewis F. and Mary Buckle. *Art in Needlework*. London: B. T. Batsford, 1907

Dedbetter, Kathryn. *Victorian Needlework*. Santa Barbara: Praeger, 2012.

Dresser, Dr. Christopher. *Penn Monthly, The*. Philadelphia: Penn Monthly Association, 1877.

Dufty, A. R. *Morris Embroideries*. London: The Society of Antiquaries, 1985.

Elliott, Bridget and Janice Helland (eds.). *Women Artists and the Decorative Arts 1880–1935*. Aldershot, Hamps.: Ashgate Publishing Limited, 2002.

Every Woman's Encyclopaedia. London: Amalgamated Press, 1911.

Fisher, Alexander. *The Art of Enameling on Metal*. London: Offices of "The Studio," 1906.

Glaister, Elizabeth. *Needlework*. London: Macmillan and Co., 1880.

Harper's Bazar. New York: Hearst Corp. May 28, 1881.

Harrison, Constance Cary. *Woman's Handiwork in Modern Homes*. New York: Charles Scribner's Sons, 1881.

Helland, Janice. *British and Irish Home Arts and Industries 1880–1914*. Dublin: Irish Academic Press, 2007.

Higgin, L. *Handbook of Embroidery*. London: The Royal School of Art Needlework, 1880.

House and Garden 1903–1910 inclusive.

The House: The Journal of Home Arts & Crafts: a Monthly for the Artistic Home. London: T. Fisher Unwin.

Hyde, Sarah. *Exhibiting Gender*. Manchester: Manchester University Press, 1997.

Kaplan, Wendy. *The Arts & Crafts Movement in Europe & America*. New York: Thames & Hudson, 2004.

King, Brenda M. *Silk and Empire*. Manchester: Manchester University Press, 2005.

Koch, Alexander. *Moderne Stickereien, Serie II.*, nd.

Larner, Gerald and Celia Larner. *The Glasgow Style*. Edinburgh: Paul Harris Publishing, 1979.

Levey, Santina M. *Discovering Embroidery of the 19th Century*. Aylesbury: Shire Publications Ltd., 1971

Levy, Mervyn. *Liberty Style: The Classic Years 1898–1910*. New York: Rizzoli International Publications, Inc., 1986.

Lewis, Gifford. *The Yeats Sisters and the Cuala*. Dublin: Irish Academic Press, 1994.

The Liberty Style. New York: Rizzoli International Publications, Inc., 1979.

Lockwood, M.S. and E. Glaister. *Art Needlework*. London: Marcus Ward, 1878.

Macbeth, Ann and May Spence. *School and Fireside Crafts*. London: Methuen & Co. Ltd., 1920.

Macbeth, Ann. *The Country Woman's Rug Book*. Leicester and London: The Dryad Press, 1929.

MacCarthy, Fiona. *William Morris*. London: Faber and Faber Limited, 1994.

MacFarlane, Fiona C. and Elizabeth F. Arthur. *Glasgow School of Art Embroidery 1894–1920*. Glasgow: Glasgow Museums and Art Galleries, 1980.

Masters, E. T. "New and Popular Artistic Needlework." *The Woman's World*, edited by Oscar Wilde. London: Cassell & Company, 1888.

Modern British Domestic Architecture and Decoration. London: *The Studio*, 1901.

Moon, Karen. *George Walton: Designer and Architect*. Oxford: White Cockade Publishing, 1993.

Morris, Barbara. *Liberty Design*. London: Pyramid Books, 1989.

Morris, Barbara. *Victorian Embroidery*. London: Herbert Jenkins Ltd., 1962.

Morris, May. *Decorative Needlework*. London: J. Hughes, 1893.

"Mrs. Traquair […] goes near enough to success in her endeavor to justify the place of honor allotted to her…". *Art Journal*, March 1903.

Parry, Linda. *Textiles of the Arts and Crafts Movement*. New York: Thames & Hudson, 1988.

Parry, Linda. *The Victoria & Albert Museum's Textile Collection*. London: V & A Publications, 1993.

Parry, Linda & Karen Livingstone. *International Arts and Crafts*. London: V & A Publications, 2005.

Rhead, G. Woolliscroft. *Modern Practical Design*. London: B.T. Batsford, 1912.

Spencer, Isobel. *Walter Crane*. New York: Macmillan Publishing Co., Inc., 1975.

Stansky, Peter. *Redesigning the World*. Princeton: Princeton University Press, 1985.

Swain, Margaret. "Mrs. Newbery's Dress." *Costume, The Journal of the Costume Society No. 12*. London: The Costume Society, 1978.

Swain, Margaret. *Scottish Embroidery: Medieval to Modern*. London: B. T. Batsford Ltd., 1986.

Swain, Margaret H. "Ann Macbeth 1875–1948." *Embroidery, Vol. 25 No. 1*. London: The Embroiderers' Guild, Spring 1974.

Swanson, Margaret and Ann Macbeth. *Educational Needlecraft*. London: Longmans, Green and Co., 1911.

Townsend, Paulson W.G. *Embroidery*. London: Truslove & Hanson, Ltd., 1907.

Townsend, W. G. Paulson. *Modern Decorative Art in England*. New York: William Helburn, Inc., 1922.

Townsend, W. G. Paulson; and Louisa Frances Pesel. *Embroidery: or, The Craft of the Needle*. London: Truslove & Hanson, 1907.

Wallace, Ann. *Arts & Crafts Textiles*. Layton, Utah: Gibbs Smith, 1999.

Wheeler, Candace. *The Art and Enterprise of American Design, 1975–1900*. New York: The Mertropolitan Museum of Art, 2001.

White, Colin. *The Enchanted World of Jessie M. King*. Edinburgh: Canongate Publishing Ltd., 1989.

Wilde, Oscar. "Mr. Pater's Imaginary Portraits." *The Pall Mall Gazette*, June 11, 1887.

Zipf, Catherine W. *Professional Pursuits*. Knoxville: The University of Tennessee Press, 2007.

The Art Journal, 1878–1908 inclusive.

The Craftsman, 1901–1912 inclusive

The Magazine of Art, 1903–1908 inclusive.

The Studio, 1897–1915 inclusive.

The Studio Year-Book of Decorative Art, 1906–1915 inclusive.

Index